PRAISE FOR *YOU ARE ENOUGH!*

" Plenty of people offer advice. Few offer wisdom. By sharing her life and experiences, Charlene Wheeless invites readers on a remarkable journey of self-discovery to gain profound insights along the way. Hers is a powerful, empowering voice and an important one for our times. This is a book for everyone. Everyone who reads this book will be enriched. "

PHILLIP BARLAG,

EXECUTIVE DIRECTOR, WORLD 50

" Charlene is a remarkable person, and there is something each of us can learn from her experience. Her stories are full of examples of her tenacity in facing the kind of adversity that comes from having to fight for everything you have, but doing it with grace, smarts, and authenticity. It is these characteristics that Charlene brought to her most difficult battle—facing and fighting cancer. For so many people, being diagnosed with cancer and dealing with this horrible disease is a transformational event. Some people are overtaken by the trauma of dealing with it, but *You Are Enough!* reminds us all that we are in charge of ourselves and that our response to and way we cope with these challenges are within our own control. So, thank you, Charlene, for the gift of these lessons and for being so brave in putting it all out there so we can apply these lessons to our own lives. "

MARGERY KRAUS,

FOUNDER AND EXECUTIVE CHAIRMAN, APCO WORLDWIDE

All those executives reading Isabel Wilkerson and Robin Diangelo to understand why their Black employees are so angry now need to add Charlene Wheeless to their bedside tables. She is a 'first Black woman to' many times over. And while she isn't a whiner and has no regrets, she offers a view of corporate America that will open your eyes. The fact that she had to confront cancer, as well, only adds to this mini-memoir's power.

ALAN MURRAY,
CEO, FORTUNE MEDIA

You Are Enough! is elegant in its straightforwardness. It is sensitively written, albeit raw. Charlene shares in a way that made me feel fully accepted as she recounted her intimate story, and also made me feel like I was intruding at the same time. The book is honest, genuine, courageous, and at all times REAL, and by the way—it is very smartly written. I loved it.

BILL HEYMAN,
CEO, HEYMAN ASSOCIATES EXECUTIVE SEARCH

This is a stirring tale of a brilliant communicator and cancer survivor who has made the most of her life in every way.

RICHARD EDELMAN,
PRESIDENT AND CHIEF EXECUTIVE OFFICER,
EDELMAN PUBLIC RELATIONS

"With a level of candor, transparency, and, yes, authenticity that will surprise you, Charlene Wheeless dispenses sound advice for living that all of us can learn from. Her personal story had already inspired me—and I know her well as a leader, colleague, and friend—but there are new details here that brought tears to my eyes and nourishment to my soul. I promise you will love this book."

ROGER BOLTON,
CEO, PAGE SOCIETY

"This book is super-relevant at any time, but especially during an unprecedented period when everyone is reassessing their lives and reprioritizing their purpose and career. Charlene's honest and reflective story of resilience in the face of serious health setbacks and refusal to accept the limitations that societal norms and conventions place on her is inspiring to everyone. She encourages women, in particular, to be their authentic selves in the workplace but to also recognize when to make pragmatic trade-offs to get results.

Everyone dreams about what might have been or what could be: Charlene's practical and down-to-earth advice tells us how to get out there and achieve our potential. As we reassess our values and respond to an extraordinary time in world history, *You Are Enough!* is the perfect guide to living in the moment and not waiting for a mythical tomorrow that never comes. It is a great primer for both work and life."

STEVE BARRETT,
EDITOR-IN-CHIEF, *PR WEEK US*

YOU ARE ENOUGH!

www.amplifypublishing.com

You Are Enough!
Reclaiming Your Career and Your Life
with Purpose, Passion, and Unapologetic Authenticity

I have tried to recreate events, locales, and conversations from my memories of them. In order to protect the anonymity of people, places, and companies, in most instances, I have refrained from naming individuals, places, and corporations and other identifying information. The content in this book is built from life and work experiences, and, in some cases, events and content from these events serve as the spark for the creation of my "Lessons." Although I provide many stories and examples in the book, they are not necessarily in chronological order. This is to prevent any intentional or unintentional identification of a workplace or a company.

For more information, please contact:
Amplify Publishing, an imprint of Mascot Books
620 Herndon Parkway, Suite 320
Herndon, VA 20170
info@amplifypublishing.com

Cover photos by Heather Philbin Photography

Library of Congress Control Number: 2020917991

CPSIA Code: PRFRE1220A

ISBN-13: 978-1-64543-586-0

Printed in Canada

To my mother, Dorthy Lockhart, also known as Bobbie Jean Long. I could not have done this without you. I am the person I am because of you. I miss you always and will love and respect you forever. To the other loves of my life, my husband, Greg, and my daughters, Jené and Savannah, you had me at "Hello."

YOU ARE ENOUGH!

RECLAIMING YOUR CAREER AND YOUR LIFE WITH PURPOSE, PASSION, AND UNAPOLOGETIC AUTHENTICITY

CHARLENE WHEELESS

CONTENTS

"What is it you plan to do
with your one wild and precious life?"

MARY OLIVER, "THE SUMMER DAY"

ACKNOWLEDGMENTS

This book is only possible because of the many people who have touched my life in immeasurable ways. Some I've known for nearly my entire life and others for a short period of time, but all are very important to me.

To my ride-or-die friend Kelly Strzelecki, who has been my sister since we first met more than forty years ago, and my favorite Monarchs, Teresa Allred Rodriguez and Kathy Stewart Love. Melissa Mauser: girl, I love you. Michael Chacon, thank you. Sheryl Olecheck, my best hot-mess of a friend, and we are forever NFL Cheerleaders without red bows.

Billy Roy Smith, you changed the trajectory of my life. I'll never know why we were brought together, but there would be no me as I am today without you. Thank you for directing me to a bigger life than I could have imagined. Dennis Grounds—*"You are too fatter than me!"* Love doesn't begin to describe my feelings for you.

Stephen Minton and Alicia Oliva, thank you for being the friends I needed and for taking me into your fold when I arrived at Texas Tech and introducing me to The Spoon. And to all my teammates on the Texas

Tech cheerleading team—Go Raiders! John Rafferty and MacArthur Stidom, you are always in my heart.

Judy and Richard Gavaghen, thank you for always being there for us through it all (and for cardboard Darius), and the rest of the *framily*. Kaitlyn and Erica, thank you for being there for my girls when they needed you most and being the other daughters I didn't even know I needed until we met. To great friends, Laura and Brian Dwinnell: thank goodness for baby monitors!

To friendships that started at work and other places and grew into something more meaningful than I could have ever imagined. Sen Sami, you are so special to me. I wish you love, light, and happiness always. Caroline Longanecker, Dawn Young, Heather Philbin, and Chuck Taylor: to call you friends is an understatement. You four are amazing. Francis Canavan, Jim Lamble, Michelle Michael, Iva Zagar, Steve Myres, Marilyn Urtubia, Michael Burke, Colton Peek, and Nick Ashooh, thank you. I would not have made it without you, your wise counsel, and your genuine friendship. Amy Ochs, thank you for drying my tears. It's been a crazy ride, but you've always been there. Kim Wimberly, thank you for spending Mother's Day and my birthday with me for nearly eighteen years in a dark auditorium! I treasure you. We raised two beautiful girls together. And thanks for figuring out how to get Greg to the right side of the store!

Philip Barlag and John Clemons—two of my favorite people whom I will always be thankful for. Philip, thank you for helping me see myself through your eyes; and to think that it all started at a car wash. John Clemons, what can I say? What us gone do?

Thank you to a cadre of some of the most amazing mentors and champions any professional could ever hope for: Paul Lombardi, one of the best CEOs I will ever know, Dan Bannister (deceased), Mike Keebaugh, and Mike Adams, thank you for believing in me. Theresa and Robert Goudie, I so treasure your friendship. Theresa, this journey would have been so much harder without you. We are forever connected.

To the great team at Amplify Publishing, especially my editor extraordinaire Kristin Clark Taylor. Wow, it's impossible to put into words what your support and encouragement have meant to me during this process. I've grown as a result of this book, and you led me to the right path at the right time and with the right words. This is our moment. The rest of the Amplify team—Naren, Nicole, Jess, and others—thank you for your support and guidance.

And thank you to the amazing team at Zilker Media. You guys are total game changers.

To my local healthcare team, Dr. Feldman, Dr. Rao, and Dr. Harnden—thank you again and again. To the healthcare team at MD Anderson Cancer Center—thank you for saving my life and giving me life. Dr. Schaverien, you are truly gifted. Thank you Dr. Tripathy for being patient with all my questions and reassuring me when I needed it most. June Grant—who knew that your fashion advice would also save my life? Thank you for your kindness, generosity, and helping me scratch things off my bucket list.

To the Comms Chicks, thank you for your camaraderie and concern and compassion: Betty Hudson, Kathy Beiser, Perry Yeatman, and the rest of the gang. Margery Kraus, my ultimate champion: thank you a thousand times over and then some. Your kindness and generosity to me can't be overstated. You are truly a gift.

There are so many other people to thank who mean so much to me that it would fill pages of this book: my friends at Reston Hospital; the Reston Chamber of Commerce; Page Society, with a special nod to Roger Bolton and his amazing dream team; Mary Elliott and Mary Boone, my Cancer Zumba support team; and my friend and personal cheerleader, Susie Harding, who kept me there and understood it all. Thank you to all my friends and colleagues who believed in me even more than I believed in myself, and to everyone who helped me along the way. A special shout-out to Steven Gaffney for giving me the push I needed and for helping me to navigate the way to my dreams.

Last, but not least, to my husband Greg, who has always been the foundation of my life for more than half my life. I love you. And my girls Jené and Savannah: you light up my life. You are the best daughters I could ever want; I am so proud of you. To my extended family: my brothers Gerald Willis (deceased) and Eric (Randy) Long. My middle brother Herman (Tony) Long, I hope you find peace and comfort. To my nieces and nephews, I am so very proud of you. Uncle Joseph and Aunt Claudette, thank you for giving me back a piece of my mother. My little Chivas Boy, the four-legged love of my life, and his side-kick Remy. Thank you for keeping me company during those late nights of writing and rewriting.

I thank God for all of you and for everything that has led me right here. Through Him, at this moment, I am exactly where I am supposed to be.

INTRODUCTION

 You alone are enough.
You have nothing to prove to anybody."
MAYA ANGELOU

I have great respect and admiration for Dr. Angelou (may she rest in peace). But nearly my whole life, and like many women and minorities, I have always had to prove myself or prove something to someone, sometimes for reasons I didn't even understand, let alone accept.

I'm tired. Fatigued, really. It's the fatigue of being excluded or made to feel invisible. In my personal life and in the corporate world, these emotional burdens have been prominent for as long as I can remember. It began as I was growing up learning how to be a little Black girl in a society that determined my value, and later as I started building my career, and later still, when I defied the odds and reached professional success. For years, I worked within the system, even if the system didn't work for me. I learned what behaviors were rewarded and how to uplift and inspire others, even as I was feeling pushed down. I mustered all the strength, fearlessness, resilience, and tenacity I could, every single day, to go along to get along. I turned myself inside out to be who "they" wanted me to be. Authenticity is great, but it wasn't paying the bills. Working hard to fit in and distancing myself from negative stereotypes—that worked. But that was before. Before I got tired. And, before I had cancer.

As I advanced in my career, I began sharing my experiences. I would speak to small and large groups of men and women about the price of exclusion and the lessons I'd learned from being invisible. Every time, the audience would start out a bit doubtful, but it never took more than one or two minutes before people were nodding in agreement, many having an acute and deeply personal understanding of the message I was delivering. Sometimes people would approach me and ask, "Why are you talking about exclusion or being invisible? What do you know about being overlooked and ignored? You're successful, and the 'big guys' like you, so what do you have to worry about?" My answer: Everything.

Just because someone has reached a level of success and appears to have shattered a glass ceiling, that does not mean they aren't experiencing blatant, conscious, and unconscious bias. It does not mean that the road has somehow become easier. That road is just *different* and often harder. The exclusion itself becomes more subtle, but it is no less painful. Each instance in isolation seems insignificant, but the significance grows with repetition. My stories, and most likely some of yours, did not unfold occasionally; they happened fairly regularly, often every day.

For me, they slowly piled up in my mind, and I found myself pushing them aside to focus on later. I learned to grin and bear it, or worse yet, to ignore what was happening because it wasn't worth it to react. Combine these forces and accumulated delay tactics, and you realize that with the repetition comes doubt. I started to believe things about myself, minorities, and women that I knew were not true. Over time, these misplaced beliefs began to erode my self-esteem and led me to question myself. If you hear or feel something often enough, you begin to believe it. The issues are systemic. Today, we call it "White privilege," and often "White *male* privilege." Here are just a few examples of how these unseen forces became startlingly visible in my own life:

- I refrained from speaking up in meetings because my ideas were frequently discounted by colleagues, only to be accepted and agreed upon when a man repeated my words a few minutes later. We've all been in that meeting when you say something you believe is important, and no one says a word or reacts. Radio silence. Then, a man repeats your words or, worse, says, "What I think she means is . . ." as though I were incapable of speaking for myself.

- I walked into meeting after meeting where other women or minorities numbered zero to three. I always counted—whether there were ten or a hundred people—and tracked when there were enough people who looked like me so that I would feel comfortable. Experts have said that gender only stops being an issue when the group of women comprise at least one-third of the audience.

- Men tended to look past or over me when standing in a group as though I weren't there at all.

- Some people discounted me because, to them, I was too young or too girly to be taken seriously only to change their behavior when they realized I was the senior person in the room. When I served as a senior vice president for a technology company, an executive colleague told me that he was pleasantly surprised that I wasn't an "empty suit." I wonder how many men had been told that? As women, we aren't allowed to be pretty and smart: we must pick one.

- And one of my "favorite" diminishments: When a man across the executive table winks at me as though to say, "Don't worry, little girl, I'll watch out for you." That's not mentoring; it's patronizing.

Maybe I did shatter the glass ceiling hindering the advancement of women, but I was to be confronted with the concrete wall; a barrier to success unique to women of color. Glass is tough, but you can break it, and you can see through it to the level above, so you know that there is something to aspire to. If you can see it, you can achieve it. Concrete, on the other hand, is impenetrable, and it blocks your vision so you cannot see how to get to the next level or even if there *is* a next level that is available to you.

So, what are we supposed to do? Give up? No. We learn to cope, and then we learn to thrive. We gain strength, and we learn lessons that give us the power and the fire to forge what's next.

Why this book, and why now?

I'm a country music fan. Well, that's not altogether true. I'm a Darius fan (country music's Darius Rucker, not Darius of Hootie & the Blowfish, although he's good, too). I have nearly every record he's made, but one of his songs stands out. The words, for me, are profound. They are my anthem. The song is "This," and a part of the chorus: *"For every stoplight I didn't make, every chance I did or I didn't take—all the doors that I had to close, all the things I knew but didn't know, Thank God for all I missed, 'cause it led me here to this."* It's actually a love song. But it hits the right chord for me and where I am in life. Everything that I have or haven't done or that has happened to me, for me, against me, or around me has led me to this moment and prepared me to tell my story.

When I was diagnosed with breast cancer in February 2017, I felt like I was at the top of my game. But I knew something was wrong. Your body tells you when it's had enough. Mine certainly did. But, like many women or people in general, I wasn't listening. I didn't stop and listen until I had to. Cancer gave me no other choice.

I didn't just decide to write a book. I felt that I *had* to write a book. I was in crisis, and as any good crisis manager will tell you, "Never waste a good crisis." I wanted to tell people about breast cancer and especially the challenges of navigating life after treatment, with most of the content coming from my blog, justbetweenusgirrls.com. The blog is an unfolding of the experiences, emotions, and feelings I encountered during my illness and immediately after cancer treatment. Its purpose was simply to help as many people as possible by giving me a platform for sharing my cancer journey of finding strength in weakness and learning to put more *life* in my life. I wanted to share my story in hopes that it would help people who had been touched by cancer in some way. I wanted to understand and help others understand the process of getting back to their old selves. (Spoiler alert: You'll never be your old self again.) I have included some pertinent blog posts after some of the chapters (edited for concision and clarity) that show you how my journey unfolded.

My publisher, of whom I'm quite fond, told me that cancer memoirs are a dime a dozen. Those may not have been his exact words, but you get my point. I cannot say that he was unenthusiastic because he was positive about the book. But what I wanted was for him to be *ecstatic*. He was not. Later, on a call with an acquaintance who is a serial entrepreneur, I was again asked about my book. This time I got a more interesting response. That is to say, he said it was an interesting idea. Then he asked the million-dollar question: "What do you hope to get out of the book?"

I thought about it for a little while, and I told him that I had a lot to say. "Like what?" he asked. I responded, "Well, there is the cancer piece and how one of the strongest women I know [me] was thrown into a massive loop of depression, self-doubt, insecurity, and a near-total loss of identity because of cancer, and how ill-prepared she was for what was ahead of her once treatment was over."

That was when the hardest work started for me. I looked for resources but felt that no one was telling the whole truth—like how after treatment, nearly everyone you run into says some version of how you must feel great for beating cancer. So, you give the proper, acceptable response and nod in agreement. Well, no, I didn't feel great. I wanted to jump off a bridge. I wanted to die, just not from cancer. I had done everything right: I fought for my life; I had both of my breasts cut off; I sat for six hours in a chair several times while poisonous chemicals were pumped into my body; I was radiated day after day for more than a month; and when I was finally ready to come up for air, I no longer remembered the life I had and didn't understand the life I was in.

"I also wanted to talk about topics that had nothing to do with cancer," I told him. Like the challenges of working as a Black woman executive where words like *meritocracy*, *diversity*, and *inclusion* are the buzz words—spoken to me more times than I can count—that in reality are too often empty and benign words. *Diversity* and *inclusion* are not words about business; they are terms about people. Every statistic is a person, a professional, doing their best to be the best and often on an uneven playing field. The Reverend Jesse Jackson once told me, "Without transparency there can be no equality. If not everyone knows the rules, the playing field can never be even." He was right then, and he continues to be right today as I type these words.

And once I thought about writing the book even more, I realized I wanted to write this book to talk about women of color at work and how the massive hidden and blatant inequities that existed sixty, twenty, and ten years ago still happen today. I want people, especially women and other marginalized and disenfranchised groups, to know that success requires a degree of fearlessness. You must be resilient for a whole lot of reasons, but it is essential if you are going to be fearless. Be tenacious about what you want. And always be authentic.

I realized that I had gotten a little carried away, but my advisor on the other end of the phone said, "Charlene, this is your book. Put all of that together and tell your story. Share your lessons because they are both career and life lessons, and you are right: people need to hear them." So, that is how this book came to fruition. I shared the new view with the publisher, and he was as close to ecstatic as I think I was going to get from him. And it was enough.

Throughout this book, I share the lessons I've curated throughout my career and life to help you push through barriers and come out the other side stronger and better. Some are profound, some you have most likely heard before, but each one has its own take, and maybe, just maybe, my view will speak to you in a new way. The relevant blog entries share how these career lessons became life lessons. They may not always seem to fit in at first, but eventually you will see their point. You see, the strength I gained in learning those career lessons also prepared me for my battle with cancer and, ultimately, my recovery. Of course, I didn't know that all this self-preparation was going on at the time over the years. As a person of faith, I've always believed the plan for my life is in God's hands and that He is always preparing me for something. I didn't know that it would be for the fight of my life when I was fifty-three and for my life after that. But here we are.

So, come and join me on this journey. The life lessons I share in this book come from me, but I want them to belong to all of us.

CHAPTER ONE

THIS IS ME

 I can be changed by what happens to me,
but I refuse to be reduced by it."
MAYA ANGELOU

Statistics have been a presence in my life from the day I came into this world. I was born in Oakland, California. We lived in Sobrante Park, a neighborhood Black families moved to in the 1960s in pursuit of the American Dream. By the time I was old enough to be aware of my surroundings—a struggling community bordered on two sides by railroad tracks—it had begun a rapid decline and was considered by many synonymous with gangs, drug dealing, shootouts, and body bags. Children could not play outside in the park for fear of being caught in the crossfire of a turf dispute or running into a drug deal. At one point in the 1980s, Sobrante Park was considered a center of crack cocaine dealing in East Oakland.

I don't remember much about my childhood. I was raised by two parents, one of them loving and protective (my mother) and one of them an angry alcoholic (my father) who liked to take his anger out on my mother verbally and physically. It does something to a kid to see the most important person in her life being physically abused repeatedly. It teaches you, or at least reinforces, what people see as the value (or lack thereof) of women. When you're that young, you don't have the mental capacity to understand what is really happening and what it all means. My oldest brother would sometimes call the police when things were especially violent, but in those days, the officers would just come into the house, briefly look around, and say something like, "Try to get along better."

I remember the sounds my mother used to make when the fights were over. They were the sounds of whimpering and misery. I will never forget those sounds, and to this day, loud voices unnerve me. Because of those experiences, I rarely raise my own voice. In adulthood, I still can't shake the feeling that loud voices signal the potential for physical or emotional violence.

Around 1971, I was one of thousands of girls in the United States who was sexually assaulted. Like so many others, something was done to me that no one has ever apologized for. It never leaves you. Worse, it's yet another lesson about the value (or devaluation) of girls in the world. You believe it's inherently your fault. It never occurs to you, at seven years old, that you are the victim. And while the aggressor goes on with his/her life, you carry the burden your entire life. There is no getting over it. Today, the Rape, Abuse & Incest National Network (RAINN) estimates that a child in the United States is sexually assaulted every nine minutes.

By the time I was in seventh grade, according to the many national statistics, I was more likely to be a teen mom than graduate from high school. But I defied those statistics. In 1981, I beat the odds by becoming the first and only person in my family to go to college, and I worked two and sometimes three jobs to be there. There were to be other statistics ahead that I could have never anticipated, too. I became a statistical anomaly; an outlier. The first Black this and the first Black female that. I've been complimented for being articulate, as though that is an accomplishment, and for being nonthreatening. I'm 5'6"-ish and 135 pounds (I didn't break 100 pounds until I was twenty-three), so how threatening could I be?

My first executive job came in the 1990s, when I was promoted to vice president of corporate communications and an officer of a multibillion-dollar company. I was not the first female to hold that job or the first female to be named VP at that company, but I was the first Black female executive there, and again at several other global companies over the years. I am proud of my achievements, but it was also disheartening that in the twenty-first century, there were still more firsts, by me and many, many other women who are more successful than me. It's isolating, being the one and only. I used to get frustrated by the isolation until I realized the importance of the achievement—that if there is one (me), there can be others. It starts with one.

My mother ultimately left my father when I was around eight years old. Broke, Black, and female, with three sons and me in tow, she just left. She worked two jobs so we could eat and have what we needed. She wasn't home much, but she did the best she could with what she had. My brothers spent more time with my dad. I spent no time with him by the time I turned ten. The next time I saw my father, I was twenty-one years old, and he told me I looked "familiar" and asked me if we had met before. The next time after that was at my mother's funeral some years later. I was married by then and pregnant with my first child. He recognized me this time, and we even took a picture together. But he was never interested in getting to know me or in being a part of my life, even though he maintained relationships with my three brothers. I never knew why I didn't matter to him. His rejection put a hole in my heart that I carried with me every day until he died in 2008. I was forty-four years old when he died, and I finally felt free. I stopped searching for the answer because the one person who could provide it was gone.

My mother was an amazing woman who worked hard so that I could have a better life. I will always drive hard to succeed because any success I achieve is for her and because of her. When people ask me what motivates me, the answer is simple: my mother. After all she endured, my success is how I thank her. It's how I honor her selflessness. How *dare* I not try my best given all she had been through for me? By her actions, she taught me to be fearless—to draw strength from knowing that my purpose was greater than my fear—and to be resilient: she did not let my father's behavior break her. She taught me to be tenacious, always. Fight for what I want. Don't give up. She never did.

And, yes, she gave me "the talk" that nearly all Black children get: "Never forget that you have to work twice as hard and be twice as good in order to be considered equal . . . and sometimes, even that won't be enough." It sounds like a cliché, but it's always been true. I've spoken those same words to my adult children. Although my mother died more than twenty-six years ago, her words and actions still affect me. They have fueled me to turn any adversity into wisdom, to be stronger than the bias, and to know when to walk away. In going to college and earning three degrees, to building a successful career, and maintaining an intact family, I am her legacy.

I should not have been surprised when I became yet another statistic in 2017. According to the American Cancer Society, I was one of 316,120 women and men in the United States who were told they had breast cancer. That's about 866 women a day who sat in a doctor's office or spoke with a doctor on the phone and, after hearing the word "cancer," heard nothing else. No doubt they were numb, even if they already suspected that it was cancer. Maybe she had someone with her to hold her hand, to be the ears that she needed at that moment. Or maybe she was alone. Out of all 316,120 women diagnosed with breast cancer in 2017, on February 20, I was concerned with just one—me.

I was in a business meeting when my phone rang. Normally, I wouldn't have taken the call, but I knew it was my doctor. I knew that I needed to take this one. I excused myself, stood in the hallway, and listened as my doctor said that yes, it was cancer. I said, "Okay." That's it, just *okay*. She said, "It's early stage, Stage 1, and there's only one tumor." I didn't know what I was supposed to do. Should I call someone? I left the meeting. Feeling tears beginning to burn behind my eyes, I went to my office, packed up my things, and went home. I called my doctor back and, always in problem-solving mode, said, "Okay, what's next?"

Over the next few days, I had several tests that gave me the definitive answer. I had Stage 2 cancer, and it had spread to my lymph nodes. I needed surgery. I was in my car, racing home to grab my luggage for a business trip. The trip was all I could think about. I knew how to have a successful business trip. I didn't know how to have cancer.

Six months earlier, I'd had a mammogram. I had a few spots that were questionable, but that wasn't unusual. There were biopsies performed, and everything was benign. I was told to go on about my business, which I did. Six months later, I was in my doctor's office again to get a referral for more tests. I needed more biopsies; a mammogram two days earlier found a few "concerning" spots. At this point, I was still more bothered than worried. After all, I had a lot to do that day. In the process of performing a quick breast exam so she could write the order, my doctor found a lump the size of a pea on my left breast near the nipple. It hadn't shown up on the mammogram. She performed a biopsy on "the pea" while I was in her office. It was Friday afternoon.

She looked concerned, so I felt concerned. Every spot on the mammogram turned out to be benign once again. But not the pea. The pea was the entrance fee to join a club that I never wanted to be a member of, and still don't. Like so many things in my life, it wasn't my choice. I tell this story because I know too many hard-charging, successful women who put off their mammograms because they are too busy with work, with their careers. I get it, but I also want to deliver this urgent message: You are never too busy to prevent your own premature death.

I have been a corporate communications professional and business executive for thirty-three years. My career choices have led me to industries that are overwhelmingly male and even more overwhelmingly White, such as oil and gas, defense, aerospace, technology, engineering—you get the point. In my last position, I led corporate affairs for a global $40-billion-a-year company, one of the most respected companies in the world in its industry. It was a great, lucrative job, and I walked away—mentally even before physically. I've been honored to receive many awards for my work and for outstanding leadership in and out of the C-suite. I always strive to be the best, achieving some level of success yet still feeling left out or that I do not measure up. To what? Usually, to someone else's idea of who I should or shouldn't be, or what I am or am not capable of, or my value as a professional and, sometimes, even as a person.

After my time in the corporate world, after a nearly three-year battle with cancer, and one visit to an Oprah event, I have reached a point in my life that has been eluding me for as long as I can remember: I have come to understand and believe something that is freaking mind-blowing. I. AM. ENOUGH. And I want you to know and feel that you are enough, too.

I close this first chapter with a blog about surviving cancer. This blog was posted almost a year after I had finished chemotherapy.

BLOG POST

Am I a Survivor?

OCTOBER 18, 2018

I've always known I was a fighter, but a *survivor*? Not so much. My mother, now, she was a survivor. She fled a twenty-year abusive marriage with nothing but a high school education and four kids in tow, the youngest being around eight (me), and she created the best life she could. That's what I call a survivor. I'm sure without her will to survive, my life would have gone in a very different direction.

Lately, I've been thinking about the word "survivor" and what it really means in context with cancer. I guess I'm thinking about it more now than usual because it's Breast Cancer Awareness Month, and everywhere I turn I see pink ribbons, pink hats, and lots of things that say "survivor" on them. With breast cancer, or any kind of cancer for that matter, I imagine it's important to identify yourself as a survivor as quickly as possible. It helps with the mental game. Some people consider themselves a survivor the minute they start treatment. Others see themselves as survivors the moment they've completed treatment. According to the National Cancer Institute, "You are a survivor on the day that you are diagnosed and throughout the rest of your life." It's a big question. One quick Google search of "Who is considered a breast cancer survivor?" resulted in 26,600,000 results in 0.55 seconds.

I think of survivor in literal terms. The dictionary says a survivor is a person "remaining after an event in which others have died." By that definition, I guess I'm a survivor, sort of. Forty-one thousand people die from breast cancer each year. I'm sure many of them thought of themselves as survivors. The problem is that for cancer people, there's always a "yet" in your head. I haven't died—yet. It reminds me of when one of my daughters was at that teenage rebellious stage. She would make a sassy statement, and I would think (and sometimes say to her), "Given the way you made that statement, go ahead and add 'dumb-shit' after it because that's what you want to say, such as 'leave me alone, dumb-shit.'" But I digress.

I'm finished with treatment, except for the revision of my first breast reconstruction surgery, and I'm on medication for the next seven years. Maybe after then I'll consider myself a survivor. But (there's always a "but"), as any cancer patient knows, cancer could come back at any time.

When I first finished treatment, people would ask me if I was all done and good as new or if I was cancer-free. The truth was that I had no idea if I was cancer-free, and I definitely wasn't good as new. The doctors went through the established protocol for treatment, and, based on that, the assumption was that I was cancer-free. Usually, I would just shrug and say, "I guess."

I visited my oncologist a couple of weeks ago, which is to say I had a medical appointment, but "visit" sounds so much nicer. Because of some strange side effects, she ordered a CT scan of my chest, abdomen, and pelvis. I guess if the cancer were to come back, that is where it is most likely to occur first. I had the scans done the following week and waited patiently for the results. Like anyone who has waited for test results, I kept telling myself that if it was something bad, she would call right away. No news is good news. Finally, I couldn't take it anymore—it had been seven days, so I called the office. Her nurse put me on hold forever (which was actually less than two minutes) and came back and said, "You're clear. There is no sign of metastasis." So, there it was, I had my answer. I was cancer-free.

Some people celebrate their "cancerversary" (cancer anniversary), which can be quite arbitrary from a date standpoint, but they do so, nonetheless. No disrespect to those who do, but I just don't see myself celebrating the day I was diagnosed or the day I finished treatment or anything else related to cancer because cancer will never be out of my life. Once you get it, you're in the club forever.

On second thought, I might celebrate something special about cancer—the day I feel that cancer doesn't define me. Sure, cancer has changed my perspective on life and most everything else, but the journey has given me the freedom to create the life I want rather than make the best of the life I had. I'll probably write on this at some point, but not today. After I've really worked it out in my head and my heart because it's deep. The day I start to truly embrace that power and create the life I want will be one of the most important days of my life, if not the most important. Now, that is worth celebrating.

I feel like I'm on the verge of it, in a good way. And, I'm making progress. I'm confident that cancer doesn't completely define me and never will. I still don't know for sure where this journey is leading me. But there is one thing I know for sure: there is no cancer in my body now. I am cancer-free!

Hi. My name is Charlene, and I'm a survivor.

CHAPTER TWO

QUIT WHINING

" It's choice, not chance, that changes your life."
OPRAH WINFREY

The words quoted above (or a close approximation) I heard Oprah Winfrey speak during a tour in Los Angeles. They're a perfect way to open this chapter of my first lesson because I want to start with a little tough love. Here goes:

Quit whining. If you don't like your circumstances, change them.
Period.

No one is coming to rescue you; it is up to you and often, you alone.

We all have that one friend (in fact, you might be him/her) who repeatedly complains about the same thing. The first few times, we listen, then we start to tune out, then we avoid the conversations (and sometimes the friend) altogether until finally, we tell him or her to either do something about it or shut up about it. Perhaps you're saying that in a nicer way, but I tend to be fairly straightforward with feedback.

In one of my first big corporate jobs, I was confronted with a dilemma. My primary role was as a writer—basically putting words on paper for the chairman to deliver to employees, managers, and other leaders—but mainly to rank-and-file employees to build *esprit de corps* or what today we call *engagement*. I threw myself into this work because I loved it. The only thing I loved more was hearing my words being spoken by the leader of the company. As a young professional, this was especially gratifying. However, at one point I realized that the words were being spoken, but the actions and decisions being made by the executives were not aligned with their words. In fact, they were completely misaligned.

It didn't feel right. More importantly, I thought it was damaging to the culture of the company. I complained to anyone who would listen and, ultimately, to my boss. Very clearly and succinctly, she said, "It's your own fault. You're the one writing the words." That's it. She put it right back on me, which is exactly where the responsibility belonged. The chairman wasn't writing his scripts, I was. Sure, as the leader of the company, he had to bear some responsibility, too, but that's not always how it works in business. In time, I became disillusioned and frustrated. I needed to shut up about it or do something. I came to realize that I had the power to change my situation. We have choices in our lives, and it is our choice that moves us forward, pulls us backward, or stagnates us. I chose to leave that job. I chose to be fearless, change my circumstances, rescue myself, and move along.

I had the benefit of being in my twenties back then, with few responsibilities and a lack of understanding of the full consequences of unemployment. I thought jobs were easy to find, and at that salary, they were. But I don't want to give you the impression that I just walked out the door that day. It took me many months to have the courage to leave and many injustices before I threw in the towel.

There was the executive who berated me in front of others for making a simple decision without consulting him first. He didn't stop until tears began streaming down my face. That situation said more about him than me, but I didn't know that at the time. There were worse things that happened. Here's an example.

A few years later when I was five months pregnant with my first child, a White male employee asked me if I was pregnant on purpose. I remember it like it was yesterday. His question showed such disrespect that it felt like a punch to the chest. To him, I was just another Black girl knocked up by a baby-daddy. I was hurt, but I was, and still am, ashamed of my venomous response back to him. I'm better than that, but his question hit me at a visceral level, and I responded accordingly. He was a bit—no, a lot—overweight, and I said, "Did you get that fat on purpose, or was it an accident?" I will openly admit that I did not say it quite as kindly. I blame it on the pregnancy hormones. That was the last straw—the reminder that I would be judged based on my skin color and gender rather than how hard I worked or what I had accomplished.

I left the company but was later asked by both the chairman and the CEO to return to the company in a higher-level position. Those two executives, both male and White, showed me that respect was possible and achievable. They went on to become some of the most important mentors and champions throughout my career. It's not that they did not see color or gender—they saw both, but they just didn't care. To them, I will always be thankful.

Changing your circumstances does not always mean that you must leave your job, but it does mean that you have to do something if you want a better outcome. I've watched people at work take new jobs or change roles or even change professions completely in order to be happier. They understood that they had the power to choose.

"KNOW YOUR WORTH. YOU MUST FIND THE COURAGE TO LEAVE THE TABLE IF RESPECT IS NO LONGER BEING SERVED."
TENE EDWARDS

As I've mentioned before, throughout my entire career, I have been the first and/or the one and only. Sometimes it's been okay, and sometimes it has been extremely uncomfortable. People would often ask me why I stayed in those situations. Why didn't I choose an easier path? Another simple answer: If I left, nothing would change. I felt a responsibility to stay. Making change was more important to me than being comfortable. It was worth it for me to stay unless the treatment ultimately made me doubt myself, who I am, my own competency, or my belief in myself. When that happens in a real way, I tell everyone, run—don't walk!—out the door as fast as you can. Once an organization begins to erode your confidence at its core, you've lost; and the only one paying the price is you.

I've spoken to or mentored many women over the years, and at some point or another, I have given them this piece of advice: *Quit whining. If you don't like your circumstances, change them.* In some cases, change hadn't occurred to them. They needed someone to give them permission, so I did. I see this often with women. Other times, and more often than I would have liked, they did nothing. They were paralyzed by fear. Fear is what keeps us from leading amazing lives. Fear makes (or keeps) us weak and wanting, but not acting. Almost every day, I ask myself, "What would you do if you weren't afraid?" Sometimes the answer surprises me. What would you do if you weren't afraid? Would you make a different choice?

Rather than complaining about what needs to change, what isn't fair, and what may never happen, recognize that it is within your control to change your circumstances. Do not let anyone ever make you think differently, or that you should wait it out. It's a job—not modern-day indentured servitude. In the end, it's not what you think about in your life that matters; it's *what you do* that counts. Don't wait for someone to rescue you: do it for yourself.

The blog post below was written nearly a year after cancer treatment when I was still grappling with understanding I had to quit whining and change my life circumstance. No one was coming to rescue me.

◆ ◆ ◆

BLOG POST

It's Complicated
NOVEMBER 10, 2018

Life is complicated. That's not a revelation, but sometimes we forget. Life is complicated. For everyone.

Over the past several weeks, my moods have vacillated between near euphoria and downright despair, and for no reason at all, really.

I blame the medication side effects. Side effects bring unwanted friends, like weight gain, quasi-depression, irritability, and sometimes an "I don't give a shit about anything" attitude, which explains why I just spent four days in London with no coat and refused to buy one. I froze my ass off but was too proud to admit it and go to the store and buy a damn coat—serves me right. I'm really over the medications and side effects. So, I took a break from them for a little while, and guess what? I feel great—like the old me again. (Depending on how you feel about me, that may or may not be a good thing!)

A few weeks ago, I spoke at a public relations conference, and as I came off stage, I ran into one of the icons of the PR industry. As he greeted me, he smiled and said, "You're back." I smiled and said I had been back for some time. He said that's not what he meant. He said he could see the light (or life) in my eyes again. I hadn't realized the light went out. I wonder when it happened. Diagnosis? Treatment? Post treatment? When I asked a colleague about it, she said there hadn't been light behind my eyes in a long time. I guess when your soul is dark, so are your eyes.

Some people see your darkness and silently pray that the real you, the whole you, will return. Some people see you in a weakened state and use it against you for their gain. And that's sad—really sad. I wonder what is so broken in them that they must break others who are already struggling?

While I was in London, I went to see the new Tina Turner musical. I just finished her latest book and was intrigued to see the show. Now, her life was complicated. She has enough perseverance, drive, and resilience for all of us. She suffered. A lot. She survived her husband, Ike Turner, using and abusing her for sixteen years and practically stalking her after she left him. She restarted a career with a bang in her mid-forties when so few people believed she could (and we all know that couldn't have been easy). In recent years, she survived a stroke, intestinal cancer, a kidney transplant, and the death of a son who died by suicide at the age of sixty. Through it all, she fought. She fought for her life, her success, and her happily ever after. And she got it. She went on to play to sold-out crowds, married the love of her life, released a book telling her story, and helped produce a musical about her life. Damn girl! Living well is the best revenge.

I wonder, though, did the light ever leave her eyes, and if so, did she know?

At the end of the show. I shed a few tears of joy for Tina. I love it when the underdog wins! I shed a few tears for me, too.

This respite from my medication will end soon, and the parts of remission I hate most will return in a matter of days. Don't get me wrong: I am truly grateful to be alive—I'm just not satisfied.

This has led me to consider going off my medication for good rather than endure it for the next seven years. A friend asked me why I would do that after all I've been through. Why would I give up now? I don't see it that way. For me, making this decision means that I'm managing my situation rather than letting it manage me. Granted, going off medication can increase the chance of cancer recurrence anywhere from 3 percent to 60 percent. I fall somewhere on the higher end (based on what I've learned from Dr. Google). Perhaps I'll see what my oncologist thinks. I know people who go off their meds without telling their doc. No judgment here, but that's just not me.

When Tina left Ike, she deliberately chose herself over anything else. She chose to change her circumstances. And it worked. Her "second act" ran circles around the first part of her life. That's kind of how I feel. Going off my medication is me choosing my life on my terms.

One evening when I was watching television, there was a scene where a psychologist (who happens to have breast cancer) is talking about people who choose to die by jumping off the Brooklyn Bridge. She says that only 1 percent survive, but 100 percent of those survivors regret having done it. She says (paraphrased): "It's not that they don't want to live; they just don't want to live like this anymore." Pretty powerful.

I feel like I'm running toward the light. Not THAT light—the one people see when they think they're dying and say God is calling them to it—I'm not running to that light. I'm running to catch up to the light that is back in my eyes where it is supposed to be. The one that is full of fire and makes me, me. I'm running to my Second Act.

In the meantime, I think I'll follow Tina's lead, and as the big wheel keeps on turning, I'm going to keep on burning—rolling, rolling, rolling down the river to living my best life, which may or may not include medication.

If going off the medication increases my chance of recurrence by less than 50 percent, it will be my choice to forego continued medication, and the key phrase in this sentence is "my choice."

My life; my rules.

CHAPTER THREE

IF YOU DO SOMETHING GOOD, TELL SOMEONE

" The working world isn't a meritocracy."

BONNIE MARCUS

Humility is overrated. I recognize that this comment is antithetical to what most of us have been told our entire lives, especially women. It is unseemly, or uncouth, or rude to tout your own accomplishments or to promote yourself. In the workplace, self-promotion is one of the greatest sins an individual, especially a leader, can commit. I get it, and I often agree. But I also know based on my experience that if you don't tell someone about your achievements, there is a good chance that you'll be the only one who knows about them, or at least the only one who remembers them when it counts.

At various times in my career, I have noticed that the people who often tout the virtues of humility and the sins of self-promotion are the people who do not need it. They are privileged. At work, they are the top executives or the people who are well-positioned in the company. They hold the keys to the castle, so to speak. They have no reason *not* to be humble; they are anything but invisible.

So, yes, for women, when it comes to your career, sometimes humility is overrated. I am not talking about shouting your wins from the rooftop, but I am talking about having the courage to own your value and learn how to make your value known. Will you be judged? Yes. Will some people speak ill of you? Probably. Will some people decide they do not like you? Yes. Will you be respected for your accomplishments? Only if people know what they are.

See if this sounds familiar to you. You start your first or new job, and whoever your advisors are—friends, parents, other relatives—say that the best advice is for you to go to work, put your head down, and do the best you can. Do not get frustrated and do not worry about everyone else; just do your work, and the boss or someone in power will notice in time. They will know you are deserving and respond accordingly. The rewards will be prestige, higher salaries, and promotions, just to name a few. Sound familiar?

So, you do what everyone else tells you. You keep your head down, you work hard, and you wait and wait—and wait—to be rewarded for your work. For someone to *notice* that you are deserving. When you look up, you see that your male counterparts, who have been working beside you from the beginning, are getting the recognition you expected to come your way. They are being promoted above you and faster than you. In the most egregious cases, they begin to treat you like you work for them. Maybe they take credit for your work, and maybe they do not even know they are doing it—or maybe they do. The result is the same. You are pigeonholed, stuck in a proverbial rut, because you are so good at what you do that they cannot possibly move you to another position. Either that, or they have no idea what you do. And, if you are not careful, in no time at all, you might find yourself reporting to the same guy who was your peer just a few years ago.

What happened? Most likely, if you are a woman, *nothing* happened. And if you are a man, you made sure that the right people knew how hard you were working. In conversation, you made sure the boss was aware of the hours you were putting in, the successful outcomes you either helped achieve or single-handedly achieved. And you were rewarded for it.

I have watched these scenarios play out again and again in my own work environments, and it has led me to the lesson that is the very title of this chapter: *If You Do Something Good, Tell Someone.* Do not rely on others to keep track of or promote your accomplishments. You have got to do this for yourself.

As women, boldly making our accomplishments known to others gets us labeled with negative descriptors like *brash, rough-around-the-edges, boastful,* and *arrogant* or worse. We know this inherently, so we take great pains to make sure we are not perceived this way. And it leaves us nowhere. We might even be concerned about being liked. Well, when it comes to work, I would rather be respected than liked. Ideally, I want both, but if I must choose, I choose r-e-s-p-e-c-t.

Well, when it comes to work, I would rather be respected than liked. Ideally, I want both, but if I must choose, I choose r-e-s-p-e-c-t.

The establishment, which can be made up of men or women in the workplace, say things like, "If she would just calm down, people would notice her work and her contributions." But that rarely happens. I have known women who have followed the rules, and yes, they did get promoted, and yes, they did end up at the top—in twenty or thirty years! Who has that kind of time? We can do better.

Early in my career, I realized the "put-your-head-down-and-you'll-get-noticed" philosophy was not a formula for success for me. In fact, it did not work later in my career, either. So, when I did something especially meaningful at work, I made sure my boss knew it, and whoever else was in charge knew it, too. And it worked for me—for a while. Perhaps because I was so young, I got a pass. As I grew in my career, however, it began to backfire. Supervisors would tell me that I came off as being only out for myself and that it was not a good look on me. I was counseled that I needed to be more subtle; apparently, people already knew that I did a good job, and I just needed to be patient and wait my turn. I heeded their advice. But that "turn" still did not come as quickly as it did for my male counterparts.

One day, I expressed this overall frustration to my husband and asked for his advice. He is a middle-aged White man (well, at that time he was younger). But, in my mind, who better to ask? At work, he was probably seen as one of *them*. He had White male privilege, so surely he would know what I should do. He suggested that I walk into my boss's office and simply let him know what I had accomplished and the value I was bringing to the company. He said, "Use facts, not stories. Don't exaggerate, but if it was your project and you're the reason for its success, say so."

So, I did. It took a while for me to get up the courage. This was not something I was used to doing, and it felt awkward. I took a deep breath and explained to my supervisor why I wanted to meet with him. I summarized the benefits and value I had brought to the organization. I had facts and anecdotal evidence, too. Let's just say it did not work out for me the way it had worked out for my husband. Instead of an acknowledgment of my worth, I was told that I was paid appropriately and should be happy because my salary was considerably more than I earned at my previous job. The behaviors that were successful for my husband did not add up to success for me. I left the meeting feeling greedy and unappreciative. I do not know if my boss made me feel that way or if I put that on myself. I mentioned my experience to a few female colleagues, and they all pretty much had the same response: Had I lost my mind? Why would I think that tactic would work for me? One colleague even implied, in jest I am sure, that I really should not try that again until I learned how to pee standing up.

I was my own worst enemy at times, but I also learned a valuable lesson: women are judged more harshly than men for speaking up about their own accomplishments. It felt like I was facing two unsatisfying options: either keep my head down and hope, or lift my head up and hope. I chose the latter.

At another company, I led an exceptionally talented team of professionals. I was enormously proud of my team and the work they did for the company and the great outcomes they produced. When it came time for my annual performance review, I listed all the things the team had done under my leadership. I was feeling good about my performance review and the opportunity to share our results. Although my performance rating was high, one of the negative comments I received was: "She takes credit for other people's work." What? I led the team, and I was reporting on our combined success—how was that taking credit for everyone else's work? When the financials of a company were solid because of the good work done by the hundreds of people who worked for the chief financial officer, was he accused of taking the credit? Of course not. He was lauded for leading a successful team.

In another instance, my team and I worked on an important project that reached across the company and had the potential to make a huge impact. The work was done by a multi-disciplinary team that included many members of my department. The leaders of the company publicly recognized the importance and value of the work, but in most, if not all, of this public recognition, every department or group that contributed to the project was commended, except mine, which was made up of all women. Again and again we were left off the public thank-you emails and left out of the recognition speech, even though we did the foundational work that directed the project. It not only felt intentional; I was convinced it *was* intentional. We were thanked privately, by the way.

Harvard Business Review articles have referred to this as a "collaboration penalty" that only exists for women, which is most pronounced when they are working with men. Studies have also shown that male workers who speak up in groups, whether pointing out problems or offering solutions, tend to emerge as leaders. Women, however, do not get the same benefits or consideration.

Even today, I still encourage my female colleagues to make their role in a project known, especially when they have done something good, and I encourage you to do the same thing. To me, the question is not whether you should speak up; rather, it is about how to speak out without penalty and being willing to take the risk. No risk, no reward.

That means we must find new ways to communicate our accomplishments and make our contributions known. It is possible to make your achievements known without sounding like a narcissist: emphasize your hard work, give credit to others, make sure you are sharing your achievements for the right reasons, and find an advocate—someone who can speak on your behalf. But choose these advocates carefully because not everyone is invested in your success. And above all else, avoid the humblebrag. According to a 2018 *TIME* article, "humblebragging" is showing off masked by a complaint. As in, "I hate that I look so young; even a nineteen-year-old hit on me!" or "Why do I always get asked to work on the most important assignment?" Humblebraggers of any gender are liked even less than out-and-out braggers.

Ask anyone if humility is overrated, and I am willing to bet no one will say yes. Well, that is okay. I say, if you do something great, tell someone about it. Be respectful. Be honest. And have the courage to claim what is yours.

I do have to add a caveat to this, however. Once you become a leader, especially an executive, any permission to self-promote is gone. Your job then is to promote the efforts of others. The balance is in promoting the efforts of others and getting your own efforts noticed at the same time, which can be tricky. This is when you need advocates the most.

This blog post below talks about a different type of courage and the power in wearing your courage on your sleeve; literally. Did people judge me for it? Yes. But I have been judged my whole life. Did I care? Sometimes, but mostly, no. The meaning for me was so much more important than any label that anyone could or did put on me about it. Somewhere in this book, you will notice a picture of me with my arms folded and a collection of bracelets on my wrist. I have been wearing those bracelets for more than two years. Here is their story.

◆ ◆ ◆

BLOG POST
Conspicuous ~~Consumption~~ Courage
APRIL 19, 2019

I am married to a modest man. Raised by a Southern Baptist Minister father and an equally religious mother, he is modest and humble. You will never find Greg donning expensive designer clothes (unless I buy them), no matter how many compliments he receives. He just does not see the value. I once found him doing yard work in a pair of awesome and expensive designer loafers I gave him for Christmas! To him, it was just another pair of black shoes. Hmmmmm. *Something is seriously wrong with this man.*

He wins awards for outstanding performance at work, and he may or may not tell me. The boasting type, he is not. When his mother passed away, I think I told more people than he did. And he waited as long as possible to let our friends and family know that I had breast cancer. So, yes, he holds things pretty close to the vest.

We are both from Texas. Well, he is from Texas. I just sort of went to college there (a story for another day). The thing is that most people I know from Texas are neither modest nor humble. They lead big, public lives. It is not so much that they are ostentatious; they just enjoy living out loud and letting everyone else see. I do not mean that pejoratively. When I went to school in Texas, my roommate drove a new convertible Cadillac. She was nineteen. I will never forget that car. I had never seen a new car before up close.

Greg has referred to this need to buy-and-boast as "conspicuous consumption." It is a clever term. He and I have had more than one discussion about my perceived conspicuous consumption. I say "perceived" because we do not agree. I think I am sharing. Humility was not really taught in my household. Bragging never came into the picture. When you are poor and Black, what are you going to brag about? Being poor and Black? I think not.

Back to Greg. Given his stance on humility and modesty, you can imagine his reaction when I started showing up with new, sparkling bracelets on my wrist. Yep, one by one, they were stacking up—and he began shaking his head. Today, there are eleven—all on one wrist—and these things are heavy! Once I asked my doctor what I should do to lose weight. He said, "Take off those bracelets."

For as long as I can remember, I have made deals and trade-offs with myself as incentives. When I run on the treadmill, I like to watch movies. If I do not finish the movie, I will not watch the rest of it until I am back on the treadmill. That was my commitment to myself—no treadmill, no movie. When our girls were little and I traveled for work, I hated being away from them. I made a deal with myself. At the end of the trip, I would buy a pair of shoes. At the beginning of the trip, it gave me something to look forward to. At the end, it signaled that I would soon be home. I have a lot of shoes.

When I was diagnosed with breast cancer, I made a deal with myself. For every milestone I faced with strength and courage, I would buy a new bracelet. If my treatment went according to plan and I showed a bit of restraint, I would have about six or seven bracelets when all was said and done. Expensive? Yes. Worth it? Hell yes! After all, my mental state was at stake.

- Cancer diagnosis, February 2017: bracelet

- Double mastectomy (BMX): bracelet and a bangle (one for each missing breast)

- Necrotic skin removal surgery on my healthy breast (complication from BMX): bangle

- Start of chemotherapy: bracelet

- Last chemo session: bracelet

- Last radiation session: bangle

- Reconstruction (the end): This bracelet was to celebrate that it was finally over.

Now come the complications:

- Breast explosion, followed by emergency surgery: bracelet

- Corrective surgery as a result of breast explosion: bracelet

- Second reconstruction November 2018: bracelet

I wear these bracelets every day, all day. I do not take them off—ever. I sleep in them, I shower in them, I exercise in them, I go through the special line at airport security for them. That is, I did until the day my acupuncturist said that they were messing with my meridian system and energy flows (Chi). He said I should take them off every night and only wear them occasionally. Occasionally? Almost all these bracelets must be screwed on in *two* places (and unscrewed)—this can take a good bit of time. He did not care. It was all about meridians and Chi for Dr. Tuan. So, we agreed that for one month, every night I would take them off, and each morning I would painstakingly screw them back on again. If I did not feel better in a month, I could wear them as long and often as my heart desired, he said. Greg thought I was crazy to do the on-off thing. People who saw me putting them on (I usually put them on while my computer was booting up or other opportune times at work) wondered aloud if it was worth it and suggested it was not. It is just jewelry, after all. To them, it is conspicuous consumption on steroids.

It has not been a month yet, but I continue with the evening and morning ritual. When I look down at my overly weighted arm, it is a reminder of what

I have been through and what I have overcome, what I have conquered, and who I am today as a result.

For me, it's not conspicuous consumption at all. It's conspicuous courage!

My month is up, but I will continue to wear my bracelets, and I will smile at people who wonder why I wear so many. I will smile at people who judge or think I am being ostentatious, and I will smile at them as they shake their heads in disapproval. They have no idea what I have been through and how I earned those bracelets. They do not think about the fact that everyone has a story. While they are judging me for something they do not understand, I'll smile and revel in the fact that I'm brave enough to be conspicuously courageous.

Everyone has a story. This is mine—and it is a doozy.

Be courageous, my friends.

CHAPTER FOUR

ASK FOR WHAT YOU WANT

> " We ask ourselves, 'Who am I to be brilliant, gorgeous, talented, fabulous?' Actually, who are you not to be?"
>
> MARIANNE WILLIAMSON

In the 1990s, I became the first Black female vice president of corporate communications and a corporate officer at a well-respected company that served the United States Department of Defense and the commercial aviation industry. The company was reaching its fifty-year anniversary, and I had recently turned thirty-five years old. I was their youngest vice president at the time, perhaps ever. As you can imagine, I was proud and pleased with myself. I had finally made it. At least, it felt that way. All these years later, I still write these words with great pride. After all, I had just grabbed the brass ring many, many years before I ever thought it could happen.

My first executive committee meeting, I was thirty minutes late. Ugh. I thought the meeting started at 8:30, but it started at 8:00. As I walked into the meeting, I immediately felt the stares and a few looks of disapproval, as though some members of the team—all male—were thinking, "See? I *told* you she wasn't ready."

Maybe it was all in my head, but it felt very real that day. As I sat at the conference table in my smart, dark-green suit, I was a little taken aback by what was happening around me. The conversation seemed important, but it was, dare I say, *normal?* I had always thought these meetings were convened to take on big challenges, like solving world peace. But it was really only regular conversation about the operations of the business. It is not that it was boring; it was just, well, boring and totally unexpected.

As I sat there in my over-sized chair, looking around, I realized that there were people in that room who had children close to my age. And I wondered what they thought: Was I too young to be there? Was I respected for my knowledge and counsel? I assume both, but that first day, I just did not know. After the meeting, I walked back to my office with the biggest smile on my face. But when I settled in my desk chair that was more appropriately sized for my small frame, my first thought was, *is this all there is?* I was proud of myself, and I was proud for all the women who were in "soft-skill" positions who would come after me, but I thought it would be different somehow. Hallowed ground or something.

A few weeks later, I asked the chairman of the company about my promotion. I was emboldened enough to remind him that I had been performing at that level for several years. I wanted to know what had taken so long for me to be promoted. What was the tipping point? He said to me, "Why didn't you tell someone you wanted to be vice president?" He went on to say that it had not occurred to them that I would want to be a vice president. I was young, I had two small children, and a successful husband. He said they assumed I was on the "Mommy Track." I never told anyone that I wanted more children, and it never occurred to them that I wanted to be on the executive track.

Here is what I learned that day: ask for what you want. If you are working toward something, make sure the right people know about it. Otherwise, you have left it up to other people to determine your future. And if the powers-that-be are more traditional in their thinking (i.e., men whose wives stayed home and raised their children), there is a pretty good chance that's the box they put other women into, as well. Sure, there are always standouts, but those were the women who were in finance or law or who ran profit-and-loss operations, not women in communications, human resources, or other similar functions.

Once I settled into my position, things became easier with most people. Surprisingly, my biggest challenges were with other senior-level women. It seemed that, in the days before Employee Resource Groups (ERGs) were widespread, other senior women could be more of a challenge than the men. You see, those were still the days when there was only room for one or two women at or near the top. Instead of helping bring each other up, the focus, unfortunately, was more on tearing each other down. I guess this was the corporate version of the movie *Mean Girls*.

After I had been in that job for a while, the company hired another female vice president. She was older than me and a bit more old-school. She ascribed to the only-room-for-one approach. She made my life exceedingly difficult, questioning my competency and attacking my credibility publicly. I approached a male senior executive with my concerns, and he said to me, "You know, we all had a bet as to how long it would be before the two of you were in a cat fight." WTF? I was speechless. I could not believe what I had just heard or even how to react to it. I just tried to focus on the problem at hand. It was clear that he was not taking me seriously at that point, nor was he taking me seriously in general.

That job and that company turned out to be one of the highlights of my career. I went on to other companies where I had greater challenges that taught me more than I could have imagined. I worked for larger companies and companies with more prestige. I learned that I can be admitted to the executive group, but not be in the inner circle and that just because you are invited to have a seat at the table does not mean you are welcome there. Acceptance was not automatic. I was very much on the perimeter of the outermost edge, and I would never be inside the circle. Not even close. But was it enough? Would it be to you? I had been admitted, but I did not "belong." But it was okay because I felt lucky to be there. Let me repeat that: *I felt lucky to be there.* Looking back on it, I am a little embarrassed that I thought so little of myself that I questioned, even briefly, if I was there by luck, rather than because of my skills, capabilities, and value.

I have talked to many women in executive positions, and all expressed some version of feeling this same way. How is it that an entire generation of smart, competent women feel that their achievement was because someone in a higher-level position decided to pluck them out of obscurity? Did we all secretly think that little of ourselves?

Further along in my career, I felt that I was paid less than what I thought I deserved. I made a handsome salary, but it was significantly less than my peers on the executive team. It was a publicly held company, so after spending about five minutes on the Security and Exchange Commission's website, you could easily figure out what the key executives were making. The next lowest-paid executive made nearly twice what I did. Was he twice as valuable? I do not know. I did not think so. But clearly, I was wrong. Call it intuition or resignation, but I knew not to question it. I was in a good situation otherwise, and it just was not worth the fight.

However, I also learned that you are never more valuable to a company than before you start. Meaning, we are never in a better negotiating position than we are before we show up for our first day of work.

I have used this approach successfully at least three times in my career, and it

A company once offered me a job and a decent salary and said that if I performed as they expected, they would increase my pay by a certain amount in six months' time. I said thank you, but no thank you. If they felt I was worth that price in six months, I should be worth it today. They came around.

helped set the stage for my steady climb up the proverbial corporate ladder. A company once offered me a job and a decent salary and said that if I performed as they expected, they would increase my pay by a certain amount in six months' time. I said thank you, but no thank you. If they felt I was worth that price in six months, I should be worth it today. They came around. Another time in an interview, the chairman asked me what it would take for me to leave my current company. I was not bold enough to throw out a number (I had not gained *that* much confidence), but I did say that the offer would have to be so good that my current CEO would say that I had to take the job. That is it. And I said it a little flippantly. Not because I was that confident or arrogant, but because I was not sure I wanted to leave my current CEO. We had grown close and were partners. We worked well together, and I felt very loyal to him. When the offer came in from the other company, it was twice my currently salary and bonus combined. I shared the offer letter with my current CEO, and he said, "Charlene, take the job." I did, and I guess the rest is history.

That CEO and I remain friends today, and I care for him and his family deeply. I learned a valuable lesson from working with him: ask for what you want. Do not wait for it to be given to you, because it may never come. If you do not ask, how will they know? But you also must be prepared for the potential downside, too—which means being willing to walk away if you do not get what you want. That is the hard part, the walking away. Men have been doing this for years. Why are we so hesitant? Because deep down, many of us women still believe we were lucky, even when we were worthy.

In work, as in life, ask for what you want.

I have carried this lesson into my personal life as well. I have learned the importance of self-advocacy and asking for what I want. Aside from work, the area where people most need to advocate for themselves is with the healthcare system. Equity in healthcare is not a given: not if you are poor, not if you are a minority, and especially not if you are uninsured.

I will admit that I am fortunate. I have some means, and I have a vast network. But when I was learning how to have cancer, I was still scared, and my means and my network weren't helpful until I learned to reach out, to advocate for myself in order to get the best care I could. When it comes to life-or-death matters—your life or death—getting the best healthcare is not an option, it is a mandate. If you are working toward something, make sure the right people know about it, be they a boss, a spouse, or an oncologist.

What's Your Number?

JANUARY 11, 2019

When I was in college and later in my early twenties, our girl posse would get together, sit around in cute pajamas or tracksuits, drink cheap wine, munch on nachos, and play one of two games—the utterly silly "Have You Ever?" or the more intriguing game "What's Your Number?"

Let me pause here to apologize to any men reading this entry—I don't mean to burst your bubble, but no, women are not wearing scantily clad lingerie and having pillow fights in slow motion on girls' night—really!

My favorite game was always the number game because it was simple. The "number" in question referred to the number of your, um, "romantic" partners to-date. It was the ultimate game of judgment. If your number was too low, you were either virtuous to a fault or there was something wrong with you. If your number was high (high being a subjective term), everyone was intrigued and wanted names and details, but in the end, you were a slut—no doubt about it. The secret of course, which we all knew, is no matter the number we nubile college girls confessed, it was not true. Everyone lied. If you wanted the truth, you took the low numbers offered up and doubled them; for the girls who gave a high a number, you divided their number by two. Looking back, it was a great way to spend girls' night, and it always led to interesting gossip that probably was not true either. Anyway, it was fun!

Now, all these years later, my number is twenty-six! Before your jaw hits the floor, you should know that I'm not talking about the old "What's Your Number?" game, I'm talking about the new "What's Your Number?" game—the one that asks my chance of cancer recurrence. When I finished treatment (surgery, chemo, and radiation), my number was thirteen. As in I had a 13 percent chance of recurrence, and therefore an 87 percent chance of non-recurrence. Now, those were odds I could live with! (No pun intended, but it is kind of clever).

So, how did I get from 13 percent to 26 percent in a matter of months? For those of you following my blog, you know that I had been wrestling with the decision to stay on my endocrine therapy medication. It made me feel awful almost all the time. Enough was enough. I had given my life over to cancer since June 2016. (Most people do not know that I was diagnosed with uterine cancer just eight months before being diagnosed with breast cancer.) Anyway, two years is a long time to feel lost, to search for yourself, and to realize you are not going to find "you" as long as that medicine is pumping through your system.

People would tell me that I just had to get used to my New Normal. Fuck that! I wanted my old normal back—and, by the way, I still wanted symmetrical boobs, too. (I got those in November!)

So, I prayed about what to do and increasingly felt like the only reasonable road for me was to go off the medication. I was tired all the time, and the weight kept piling on. I had control over nothing, it seemed. I could not live like this for another seven to ten years.

The praying helped put me at ease, but just in case, I went to see a spiritual reader. Yes, you read that correctly. She got decent reviews on Yelp, so I figured, why not? Plus, it would be interesting to know what the universe thought about all this cancer business. This lady was bona fide crazy! But she told me what I wanted to hear: "Your cancer isn't going to come back." Well, if she said it, it must be true! I decided to believe her.

I talked to my doctor about it, too. Well, truthfully, I sent her an email; I was worried that if I spoke to her, she would try to talk me out of it. She said the protocol is what it is, and we could try different medicines until we found the right one. But in the end, she supported my decision. People have to weigh quality of life over quantity of life, she said. On the bright side, I am thrilled that my Google search was wrong in calculating my chance of recurrence at slightly north of 60 percent but seems to really be 26 percent. *Math has never been my strong suit.*

I then began to read books about managing cancer risks metabolically and through lifestyle changes. One book, *Anti-Cancer*, by Dr. David Servan-Schreiber really spoke to me. I read it twice. I learned that there are foods that feed your cancer and foods that cause cancer cells to die. So, I have changed how I eat, exercise, and drink (most of the time). And I have never felt better. At least not in a long time.

Except . . .

Except, when I stop to think that by making this choice, I have also chosen to perhaps miss the wonderful times ahead. Like when my girls get married, then have children, and those children call me G'ma Charlie. I might not be there to watch my girls turn into mature adults or give them advice and help guide them through the tough times. I wouldn't be there if Greg passed away early, peacefully, in his sleep one night, leading me to hook up with some eighty-five-year-old billionaire—someone one old enough to think I was a cute young thing but too old to do anything about it! That last one is a joke of course. I adore my husband.

My mother died a couple of years after Greg and I married. She never met my girls, although I see her in them all time. She was not there to guide me through anything. She was sick, and she died. There was a time when I resented her for dying on me even though I knew it was the best thing for her and she had no control of it, anyway. None of us do, really, I suppose. But if I am not there for my girls, will they resent me for it? Will they feel like they were not enough to keep me fighting? Will I have made an incredibly selfish decision? Will I have disappointed them?

It is heady stuff. And, it turns out I am not alone. Nearly 25 percent of women choose to forego endocrine therapy and take their chances. They do not want the crazy side effects of mood swings, joint pain, broken bones, nausea, hot flashes, and the list goes on. They want their lives back, too.

But, alas, while engaging in all this pondering and reading, I came across a recent study that said women with my type of cancer who did the "right" thing and stayed on endocrine therapy for the requisite amount of time still were not free and clear. According to Dr. Jennifer Litton at MD Anderson Cancer Center (the best cancer center ever!), "Many women think 'Okay, I have made it to five years, I know I'm safe.' But for estrogen-receptor positive breast cancer, [recurrence is] a continued lifelong risk."

Well, damn.

CHAPTER FIVE

EVERYONE NEEDS A CHAMPION

> " Unconscious bias determines who gets to play
> and who sits on the sidelines."
> REV. JESSE JACKSON

Mentors help you learn; champions save your job. I should know. I was single-handedly the cause of very unflattering information about the chairperson of a company I worked for being published in a global business magazine. I worked with the media at the time, and I collaborated with a reporter on a profile of the chairman. In communications circles, this was a huge win! I just knew this "hit" was going to launch me at this company.

I spoke to the journalist nearly every day. I worked with the chairperson on talking points and messages. I worked with the photographer to make sure we captured the perfect photo. After more than a month's work, the journalist called to let me know that he had sent the finished piece to his editor and that the article should be a two-to-three-page feature. I was so excited I could hardly contain myself! I told everyone; the chairman told his friends. Finally, publication day came. I bought the publication and scoured it for the article. The "three-page article" had been reduced to a one-paragraph story! The worst part was that the one-paragraph started with "We can fire 'em," referring to how we handled our employees if our workload changed due to the loss of a project, and ended with (paraphrased), "not bad for a man with only a high school education."

Up to that point, few people knew that our chairman had not gone to college. He was a self-made man and well respected, but he was also particularly sensitive about not holding even an undergraduate degree. It did not come out in the interviews; the editor learned it during the fact-checking process. There was no way around it. In hindsight, I am glad the big search engines like Google and Yahoo! were not household names just yet.

As you might expect, the chairman was livid. He wanted me fired that day. Someone had to be the fall guy, and it was going to be me—that is, until my boss, my champion, stepped in. She explained the workings of the media and that no matter how hard we try, we ultimately have no control over what is printed. And let us not forget, the statement itself was accurate. She talked him off the ledge, so to speak, and in the end, I was able to keep my job. The article did not launch me anywhere—I was just thankful to still have a job.

That is when I learned the difference between a mentor and a champion. Many people consider the roles synonymous, but over the years, I've experienced a divide. Mentors advise you, point you in necessary directions, and help you learn about your company or business in general. A champion, on the other hand, is the person who is looking out for you: the senior person who is in the room when critical discussions are taking place and decisions are being made. Champions are the people who speak up for you when you do not have a seat at the table; your voice when you have no other way to be heard. Think of it this way: a mentor is your advisor, but a champion is your *advocate*. Most importantly, champions make sure that the people who need to remember you, do. Champions have influence, and they are not afraid to use it. And perhaps most importantly, champions can break through unconscious bias even when you do not know it exists.

In focusing on champions, I am not disputing the need for or value of mentors. I believe mentors play an important role in a person's development. I have had the honor of mentoring many young men and women throughout my career. It is certainly my hope that I provided value to them and gave them tools that served them well. Everyone should have a mentor, and often more than one, male and female.

I have had many mentors over my career, but few champions. Whenever I have had a champion, I readily admit that my job was easier, being recognized for my value was easier, my ability to be *me* was easier. With a champion, I had hope for my own future and hope for my future in the organization.

There was a time I had powerful, well-positioned champions in my corner. But my champions retired—all of them—and I did not have backups. Slowly but surely, I watched my career circle the drain. Without champions, people perceived me differently: what they once saw as my ability to "think outside of the box" was now being seen as me not understanding the business. My willingness to speak up and speak out became me not being a team player and not knowing my place. It was the first time I had experienced what I call "corporate whiplash." For years, I was on top, but over a matter of months, I was not anymore. It was swift, painful, and confusing. It is one thing to have to prove your value at work; it is another when no one *cares*. Ultimately, I figured out my place: it was at a different company.

Not surprisingly, men figured out the power of champions a long time ago. According to Sylvia Ann Hewlett, an economist and author of *Forget a Mentor, Find a Sponsor: The New Way to Fast-Track Your Career*, male professionals are, on average, 46 percent more likely to have a champion or sponsor than female professionals. It is one way they are able to move up in their careers quickly. Additionally, Whites are 63 percent more likely than professionals of color to have someone at the decision-making table backing them. Where does that leave women and people of color? In catch-up mode—and at a distinct disadvantage.

Bottom line: if you want to get ahead, get promoted, or get noticed, get a champion. In fact, do not seek out just one. Find *several* so that you do not find yourself in the same situation as I did. Today, I like to think of it as building my own personal army of advocates. The key to making this happen is through building strong, sustainable relationships. There is no magic bullet, but there *is* magic in having a champion.

One of my strongest champions is an amazing, thoughtful, and powerful woman, although she probably would not describe herself that way. She is also founder and executive chair of a global advisory and advocacy firm—the largest global firm that is majority female-owned. She has been a career champion for me for nearly a decade. With her help, I rose from near anonymity in my professional industry to one of its best-known leaders.

Keep in mind that champions work both ways. Most champions want to advocate for someone they believe is going to put in the work to be

> Bottom line: If you want to get ahead, get promoted, or get noticed, get a champion.

successful. Champions look for people with credibility, confidence, and consistency because champions do not just speak up; they open doors. Champions can come from the strangest places, and they can show up when we least expect it. Find your champion, and if you already have one, be a champion for someone else. Everyone needs a champion.

There are so many career lessons that when put into practice in my personal life made a significant difference. In some cases, the difference was literally life or death. Of course, I am talking about my *own* life and death.

After I finally understood what it meant to have cancer, I did not know which way to turn. I went to see three oncologists, a breast surgeon, my primary care physician, and anyone else who would see me who could provide answers. And I was scared. If I had taken the time to think about my network, I am confident I would have been able to identify some of the best resources in the country to help guide me. But those were the days that I thought asking for help was synonymous with weakness. And when you grew up the way I did, you never like to show weakness.

> Champions look for people with credibility, confidence, and consistency because champions do not just speak up; they open doors.

One day, I reached out to my friend and champion to ask about cancer. She connected me with a highly respected doctor in Houston, Texas. In a matter of days, I was in Houston speaking with one of the nation's best breast oncology teams. At that appointment, I was told for the first time—and the only time—words I really needed to hear: "This is curable."

With this team as my personal advisors, I moved forward with my treatment in my home state of Virginia. But after completing all the invasive parts of breast cancer treatment and completing breast recon-struction, my breast "blew up," and I almost died. I made it to the hospi-tal in time, but it was clear that had I not, I would have bled to death. I am prone to side effects.

Again, my champion got involved. Less than a week after the "explo-sion," I was back in Houston in the office of a renowned breast recon-struction surgeon who was, I believe, one of only a few doctors in the world who could have addressed my problem. And he did.

You may not know when, where, how, or why at the time. But everyone needs a champion.

◆ ◆ ◆

The Spontaneous Combustion of My Breast

AUGUST 18, 2018

I have been doing well—getting back into the swing of things and feeling good, if not great. But alas, sometimes three steps forward come with two steps back.

Just when you think you have kicked cancer's ass, something happens to remind you that you have not gotten there—not yet. Damn.

On Sunday night, June 3, 2018, I arrived in Texas full of vim and vigor to attend an industry conference I had been looking forward to for some time. I missed last year's conference due to being in treatment. I got up on Monday feeling cute as ever in a white/green/gray zip-up Akris

Punto dress and white Dior pumps that I just love! Stay with me, they are pertinent to the story. I head down to breakfast, hug a few friends, and sit down to eat. Almost immediately, my chest began to tighten, and my left breast (the one with cancer) had started swelling—I mean really swelling, really fast.

Within thirty minutes, it had swollen under my arm and nearly to my collarbone and was at least three times bigger than when I got up that morning.

I call my doc's office in Virginia, and his nurse says, "Get to the emergency room." So, I call an ambulance, and they take me to the nearest hospital. At some point, I call my husband, Greg, and tell him what has happened. Anyway, on my arrival to the emergency room, my blood pressure plummets, and I am fading in and out. All I can hear is the nurse telling me to stay with her and shaking me awake. She does not want me to pass out. I cannot keep my eyes open. I just want to sleep, but I try my best. At this point, my breast is still swelling, and I am still in my dress, praying they do not try to cut me out of it. I mean, this dress was an investment! She tells me that I need to sit up so I can get out of my dress. I say I cannot, my breast is going to explode. She thinks I am kidding.

I unzip the front of the dress, she sits me up, and sure enough, my breast explodes. I mean bursts open. Blood is *everywhere*, including all over the front and back of my dress and my shoes. The explosion is so large that my brand-new implant comes out and falls to the floor intact. Undamaged! It becomes clear pretty quickly that my implant did not explode, my skin did from the pressure. It turns out my reconstruction scar of four weeks ago that had completely healed gave way to my blood-filled breast. Everyone is horrified, even the ER doc and the three nurses who are staring at me. No one does anything for a few seconds, so I say, "Shouldn't we put compression on this before I pass out?" They snap out of it, put compression on the "wound," and I pass out as I hear them say to prepare for a blood transfusion because I have lost so much blood. I still do not know if I had a transfusion. I have on a bracelet that says I might have. Who knows?

By now, the bleeding is controlled and so is my blood pressure, so they start giving me IV meds (no idea what) and prepare to transfer me to another hospital. This one doesn't have a plastic surgeon on staff, and I need surgery right away. Seriously?

I get to the new hospital, and the (gorgeous) plastic surgeon says, "I've never seen anything like this. Never." He calls my doc in Virginia; they doc-chat for a while and determine surgery is a must, first thing in the morning. He says a blood clot is the worst that can happen, but he doubts that will occur. He takes another look at the wound. Now, I don't know about you, but I've been to so many doctors lately that when they look at me or my situation, I don't listen to what they say, I watch their eyes and often their facial expressions. Sometimes doctors give away a lot and do not mean to. As the cute doc looks at the wound, he cringes. I kid you not—he cringes. This cannot possibly be good. Of course, it has not been good yet, so why should it start now?

A dear friend, who is also at the conference, ignores my protests about her visiting me at the hospital and comes anyway (thank you) to keep me company until my husband arrives. Yes, my husband hops on a plane to Texas—this must be serious. What you need to know about my husband is that he is a steady, serious guy. He is not the one to run to your bedside and sit there holding your hand while they put in an IV. He is more the "I love you, and tell me if you need anything" kind of guy, but not in a cold way—just a matter-of-fact way. He arrives around 9:00 pm, and I am so glad to see him. If he is here, I know it is serious, but I also know that it is going to be okay. No one could possibly advocate for me or take better care of me.

The next morning, surgery goes as planned. Except, I wake up with only one breast. Really. The other one is gone, gone, gone. This is shocking to me.

The next morning, Greg and I (and just my right boob) are flying home. Tomorrow, I will see my surgeon in Virginia and determine the next steps for my mutilated body. He thinks there are options.

What I would do now for those two oddly, but not horribly, reconstructed breasts I had just a month ago. The journey I thought was ending seems to only be in the middle—the fifth inning and not the ninth. I hope that makes sense (I do not follow baseball).

I am reminded that people always tell me that I am resilient. I guess I am. I just hope in the end people will say that I rallied; I always tried to be positive, even when I felt my resolve crumbling.

◆ ◆ ◆

BLOG POST
Part Two: The Rest of the Story
SEPTEMBER 1, 2018

The day after we returned home, I went to see my doctor in Virginia. When he walked into the room, he said, "So, your implant burst?" I said no, it did not. I had a feeling that was what the other doctor would tell him, so I reached into my purse, pulled out my implant, and put it in his hand. I had asked the nurse in the emergency room if I could keep it. He was surprised that I brought the implant back with me. "You kept it?" he said. Admittedly, it was a little odd. I told him that I wanted to be clear that the implant had not ruptured and that I did not trust that the ER doc would accurately convey that information. I was right.

Not one to criticize another doctor's work, he just said it would be okay, that I should rest for a week, and the implant could be put back in over the next two weeks. That did not make sense to me. Hadn't I lost skin in this process? Was I getting new skin? Cadaver skin? He was onto the next patient before I could gather myself to ask those questions. To be clear, I trust this doctor, and I am not one to second guess him. So, I rested for a week and was scheduled for the reimplantation on June 21. I decided that in the meantime, I would remain lopsided. No chicken cutlets for me! For some reason, stuffing my bra on top of all of this was just one step too far.

My uneasiness led me to cancel my surgery and seek out another path. I just had a nagging feeling I needed to do something else. Over that weekend, I got a call from one of the senior executives at MD Anderson Cancer Center. They arranged for a team to see me in just a few days. I flew to Houston and learned more about what happened. What is consistent is that it is rare: only two people (including me) had something similar occur, but only one blew up—me.

If you are wondering what happened to the Akris Punto dress, my husband took it to the dry cleaners, and they said no way, no how. I think there was some concern about it being a biohazard and/or they thought he had committed a gruesome murder and was trying to get rid of the evidence. Either way, they were not touching it. But all was not lost. He soaked the dress in cold water in the bathtub at the hotel for more than an hour and carefully pulled out all the blood clots. *Gross!* If that is not love, I do not know what is. The dress is now good as new, and the only remaining stain is on the inside label. A subtle reminder of life, death, love, and resilience.

Oh, and in case you are wondering, this whole episode was worth **two** bracelets.

When I started this bracelet-milestone project, I was so excited! I thought I would be glancing at my wrist, smiling in awe because it would remind me of what I have overcome and how strong I was, like Almighty Isis (the female superhero) or something. Instead, at least for now, I look at my wrist, and it just reminds me of all the shit I have gone through and the shit that awaits me. I sound bitter, I know, but I am not. I am just very, very tired, and I do not know when the end will be in sight.

Re-reconstruction is scheduled for November 13, 2018!

One more thing about that Akris Punto dress—this is where fashion helped save my life. The fabric of the dress was so thick, it served as a compression garment up until the zipper was released. It kept me from bleeding to death—seriously.

CHAPTER SIX

STEP UP!

" The question isn't who is going to let me; it's who is going to stop me."

AYN RAND

While I have learned the importance of speaking up and asking for what I want, there is a corollary to that lesson that I still struggle with sometimes. Not only do we need to speak up and ask for what we want, we need to *Step Up!*—sometimes in a big way. The most important lesson in this chapter is to not be afraid to venture outside of your comfort zone. And never, ever let anyone tell you what you can or cannot do. Take the risk, and then reach higher.

By now, it has been well documented that women find it hard to believe in themselves and, as a result, are hesitant to take on work or even apply for jobs for which they feel they are not 100 percent qualified. Several years ago, Hewlett-Packard issued a then-groundbreaking internal study noting that men will consistently apply for a job even if they meet only 60 percent of the qualifications. Women, on the other hand, usually do not apply for new jobs unless they are certain they meet *all* the qualifications. We women are right in one way. A more recent McKinsey study revealed that men are often hired or promoted for their potential and women are hired for their experience and track record. Human resource professionals will tell you that the job description is a "wish list." Women tend to see them as absolute rules; men see them as guidelines. Why the difference?

Study after study will reveal that men are good with the 60 percent because they are fully confident they will figure out the rest once they get there. We women, on the other hand, are worried about being *found out* or revealed as inadequate, and we struggle with the feeling that we do not belong. This is also known as the "Imposter Syndrome" (IS). IS, which was first identified by psychologists Pauline Clance and Suzann Imes in 1978, is defined as a mixture of anxiety and a persistent inability to recognize one's own worth. The psychologists also found that both men and women suffer from IS, but it's typically more debilitating for women because we tend to surrender to our own self-doubt; we tend to internalize and validate the negative chatter that runs through our brains. So, hear me clearly on this: *when you criticize yourself, you undermine yourself.* And trust me, there are enough people in the workplace looking to undermine you; you do not need to add yourself to the mix.

I have had IS for most of my life. I have always been afraid of being "found out". I wasn't sure exactly what there was to find, but that did not keep me from living in fear. Pretty much every day I thought I was going to be fired. It is not rational, but it made sense to me. I have spoken with other executive women who feel or have felt the same way. It is like we cannot quite get our footing. We sometimes laugh about it, but the reality is that it is not funny at all. Your career is not laughable. Such self-doubt and constant fear can be crippling.

In a study by Tara Mohr, author of *Playing Big: Find Your Voice, Your Mission, Your Message*, women said their main reason for feeling such anxiety was that they were afraid of failure. One subject of the study said, "I didn't think they would hire me, since I didn't meet the qualifications, and I didn't want to put myself out there if I was likely to fail."

It turns out there is a good reason for this concern. There is some evidence that women's failures are remembered longer than men's. If you are a woman of color, specifically Black, the stakes are even higher. As author and blogger Luvvie Ajayi says so eloquently, "Our failures are considered the rule, and our success is considered the exception."

I have built almost my entire career on this thought—if failure is the rule, I will win through the element of surprise. As author and cartoonist Lynda Barry once said, "Expect the unexpected, and whenever possible, be the unexpected." This thinking carried me through a life where my "Blackness" was often implied or blatantly called out as an issue. In each decade of my life, when I began to feel confident and secure, something would happen to remind me that society had not overcome racism just yet. Challenges based on my race would always be with me.

When I was around eleven, in seventh grade, I tried out for the cheerleading team and made it as the fourth alternate. Do you know how bad you have to be to be chosen as the fourth alternate? Pretty bad. Of course, I was disappointed because I thought I had at least a little talent. To my surprise, I was put on the team within a few months! The sponsor (we did not have coaches in those days) told me I did not make the team when I first tried out because I was Black, and they thought I would be a troublemaker. I guess after being at the school for a while, they saw that I was not who or what they expected. At the time, my eleven-year-old self was hurt, but the saddest part about it was that I actually *understood* their decision. Even now, I cannot believe I bought into the whole thing.

And there was the time in college when I walked into a record store to buy a new single that I loved to dance to at a local bar with my friends. I knew the name of the song but not the name of the band. The manager and a sales associate at the store were trying to help me find it. They must have spent ten minutes looking for this record. Finally, they gave up, and the manager told me that the song did not exist on the "Hot Black Singles" charts. I just looked at him in surprise and disappointment and said, "I never said it was a 'Hot Black Single,' before walking out of the store, irate and hurt. In case you are wondering, the name of the song is *West End Girls* by the Pet Shop Boys. (Do not judge me for my musical tastes; I was only about twenty years old!)

After I joined the work world, I was invited to go through a week-long management training session sponsored by my company. One day of the training was dedicated to being coached in public speaking. One of the exercises required every participant to stand in front of the group and give an impromptu speech for about five minutes on a specified topic. The point of the exercise was to put us on the spot and see how well we performed. The instructor made a point of giving us topics that she assumed we probably did not know anything about. The idea was to catch us off guard—and did it ever!

When it came to me, the instructor said under her breath, but loud enough for us to hear, "This is a good one." She gave me the topic of country music. Being Black does not mean you do not listen to country music. I happen to know enough about music to riff for at *least* thirty minutes on many different types, including country—*especially* country. The weekend before the training, my husband and I had taken our girls to see Taylor Swift, who was the opening act for the headliner Rascal Flatts. When I finished my impromptu (and very well-informed) remarks, she responded with a weak voice and a raised eyebrow, "Well, *that* was unexpected." Maybe to her. But not at all to me.

And, on an even more personal note, when Greg, who is as white as Wonder Bread, told his parents that we were engaged, his mother practically begged him not to marry me. This was 1991, not 1961! She was clear that a Black wife was not her idea of the best choice for her baby boy. She always wanted him to marry an educated, kind, Christian girl. I used to joke that she should have been more specific and said that she also needed to be *White*. But there was a lot of hurt hiding behind that joke. My husband chose to follow his heart. As I write this book, it brings me much joy, much pleasure, and much pride to write that we have been married nearly thirty years and have two, beautiful mixed-race daughters.

My mother-in-law never really came around before she died, but I am blessed that my father-in-law, a retired Southern Baptist preacher, officiated our wedding and conducted a beautiful ceremony. He had a booming voice, and during proceedings, as Greg and I stood at the altar holding hands, he sang the hymn "Wedding Prayer" acapella. Even now, I remember it as a powerful and poignant moment. Just thinking about it brings tears to my eyes and a deep feeling of gratitude in my heart. To him, I will always be thankful and will always honor him for having no expectations, except that I would be a good wife to his son. He is in his nineties now, and I have not ever heard him say anything unkind about Greg and me as a couple or our family of four.

So, I know a little something about being unexpected. But, I digress yet again. Let me get back to the real point about how we women manage, drive, and sometimes even derail our careers. If women's failures are remembered longer than men's, it means we pay a higher price, which means, in turn, that we need to look at our relationship with failure much more closely.

To me, suffering from a lack of confidence and a fear of failure, particularly public failure, are just two sides of the same coin for women. I know from experience that we learn more from our failures than we do from our successes. It is a popular refrain among leaders, but I have always found it difficult for male leaders to easily point to a list of successive failures that derailed their careers. In my experience, men often *fail upward*. We have all seen it at one time or another: a male employee makes a big mistake, and the sentiment is that he learned a valuable lesson. Before you know it, he is promoted into a higher-level position. In general, women do not fail upward. We just fail.

Here is the bottom line: It is past time for women, and especially women of color, to be promoted or hired for our potential *and* our expertise. We must be willing to take that extra risk and move beyond our comfort zones to do something we have never done before. Take on a job with confidence and courage, regardless of prior experience, and like our male counterparts, we must know and believe that we will figure it out once we get there.

During the 1980s and early 1990s, nearly everyone in the business world was talking about and completely enamored with the latest craze for ensuring that a company delivers quality products and services through continuous improvement, and you could certainly count my company among those who bought into it hook, line, and sinker. The initiative required that thousands of employees be trained on the quality practices. The most efficient way to do this was to train a cadre of employees who could then train other employees. These efforts are often referred to as "train the trainer" sessions. Our Head of Quality at the time was responsible for recruiting leaders to be trainers. One day, I mustered up the courage to ask him about becoming a trainer in the company in addition to my full-time role in communications. He said no, adding that women trainers often come off as sounding condescending, and given that my company was primarily older and male, there was some concern about my ability to be effective. He did not say that, exactly, but you could feel it in the air. I was not going to be deterred. It was my opportunity to *Step*

Up! I just felt that it was something I was meant to do, and it suited my career needs at the time: being a trainer would provide greater exposure to the business and allow me to build broader, stronger relationships with leaders who were outside of corporate headquarters. Additionally, by meeting more people from all parts of the company, I felt it would enhance my ability to perform my current job. As far as I was concerned, it was a win-win-win. However, I was about to learn another important lesson: with stepping up comes visibility and credibility—two crucial characteristics in business. It is a lot harder to succeed if people do not know you exist.

A few weeks after the turn-down, which only served to further embolden me, I was working with the chairman who also happened to be the executive sponsor of the quality initiative. I mentioned to him casually (or perhaps it was cautiously) that I thought I would be a good trainer for the effort, and that I would like to give it a try. I recognized that I was going over a superior's head, which was ballsy as hell, but in my mind, the quality manager was not my boss, and I was trying another route to reach my goal. Really, sometimes you just have to take the risk.

> It is easier to ask forgiveness than seek permission.

It is often easier to ask forgiveness than seek permission. The chairman said yes and that he would make sure it happened. Before I knew it, I was being trained as a trainer, traveling around the company teaching courses, building relationships, and learning about the business. Turns out, I was not condescending in the least; in fact, I was fairly good at training. I loved it. I went on to perform this extra work for another two years or so before I left the company. In the end, did it work out for me? Yes! That is the same company where I became a corporate officer at thirty-five years old.

But, the biggest *Step Up!* for me came when I was a communications executive at a different company. Within the company's organizational structure, someone was assigned to be the lead executive at each of its largest locations. It was not a full-time job, but it was recognition of your leadership. The role was always held by someone on the operations side of the company, which involved the running of the business. It was more than facility maintenance and management; it also included employee morale, government audits, overseeing some manufacturing, supply chain, security, and other functions. All things I knew nothing about.

One day, and seemingly out of the blue, the president of the business unit I worked in asked me to take on the role. At first, I was taken aback. Then I thought "Wow, this is really cool!" And *then*—you guessed it— the all-too-familiar fear and anxiety set in. All these emotions unfolded within about five or ten minutes. Finally, I said to him, "You do know that I do not know anything about these functions, right? I'm a communications person." Now, let me say this again: *Never sell yourself short.* Even if you think it is justified. When you criticize yourself, you undermine yourself.

He told me that he understood but believed in me and my ability to lead and learn, and he thought I could do the job. I finally agreed and asked if it came with additional pay. He said it did not. But that was not a deterrent because it was still a great opportunity, and I felt lucky to get the additional assignment. It never occurred to me that it was more than just luck or that I had *earned* the opportunity and *deserved* the additional responsibility and recognition. Many successful women will tell you that a fatal flaw for all of us is accepting additional responsibility without additional pay. For men, it is almost always, "Show me the money," yet for women it too often seems to be, "Thank you, and I promise I'll do a good job for you."

When my additional responsibilities were announced, people were surprised. In the company, I was the first non-operations person and communications leader to be in that role. I figured out how to make it work. I built a leadership team and interacted with the government and the customer and whomever else I needed to. I studied hard, worked hard, developed new employee programs, held town hall meetings, and launched a site-wide employee morale initiative. I spoke to women's groups and talked about the importance of "the stretch"—which is reaching beyond what you think you can accomplish. And when I left the company for another opportunity elsewhere, the employee feedback I received was all the acknowledgment I needed to know I had made a difference. Before I left the company, another woman who worked at my location sent me an email to tell me that she, too, was leaving the company. She had applied for a job for which she did not feel fully qualified, but after attending one of my talks about believing in yourself, she decided to apply for it anyway, and she got the job. She told me she would have never done it if she had not learned the importance of having the courage to step up and out of your comfort zone. So, I'll end this chapter the same way I began, with not so much a request as a mandate: If you want to succeed, if you want to push past your own fear, if you want to sidestep your own self-doubt, then *Step Up!*

CHAPTER SEVEN

FIT MATTERS

" Why fit in when you were born to stand out?"

DR. SEUSS

I have been giving the talk about lessons I learned from being invisible for many years. Each time I prepare for the intended audience, I review my lessons to make sure they are still relevant and that they resonate. Sometimes I change up the words a little, customize them appropriately for each audience, but the underlying messages are pretty much the same throughout, just as they have been throughout this book: you are not alone. We have shared experiences, and we are not going to be invisible anymore.

For more than fifteen years, I have talked about "fit" in the context of fitting in at work. And I have proudly and repeatedly said that, yes, fit matters. But it does not have to mean that one size fits all. There is still room for variance and diversity. I tend to think I am living proof. I am hard-pressed to name a company for which I have worked where I, or others, would consider me a *natural* fit. I have always worked at places where people who looked like me were few and far between. Yet, I was still able to achieve a successful career by most standards. I have been able to avoid what some organizations have referred to as "organ rejection," which is what happens when the majority body of the organization senses the presence of a foreign object (me) and squeezes it out, suffocates it, or simply rejects it outright. Just like in human organ transplantation, being a transplant in an organization does not always work. Sometimes the body rejects the foreign object, leaving the new host broken. I know a bit about organ rejection, personally and professionally.

My mother had a heart transplant when she was in her mid-fifties. However, within a year, despite the many drugs she was given to support organ acceptance, her body began to reject the new heart. Slowly, the heart beating in her chest and keeping her alive began to fail. The doctors said that without a second heart transplant, she would die. After spending nearly a year in the hospital, my mother was sent home. The doctors had lost hope that the donor heart she needed would become available in time, and my mother wanted to live out her last days in her house. She was ready. All the possible interventions had been exhausted.

One evening, in the middle of the night, my mother called me. (I lived in Washington, D.C., at the time, and she was in Albuquerque, New Mexico.) A heart had come available, which meant, of course, that someone had died, and his family made the generous decision to donate his organs. His heart went to my mother. She called to tell me that the heart was a match, that she'd gotten her "Hail Mary." She told me she was headed to the hospital, that she loved me very much, and that I would see her when she woke up. She was crying tears of joy as she spoke; we both were. Given the length of the surgery, I had enough time to fly to Albuquerque and make sure I was standing at her bedside when she awoke. But I did not go.

Somehow, I just *knew* that the transplant was not going to work. I don't know how I knew, but I did. And, I especially did not want to walk off the airplane and be greeted by a family member who came to tell me my mother had died. And I was right. When the doctors removed my mother's failing heart and placed her on life support while they prepared the new heart for its new home, they discovered the donor heart had died sometime between transport and the planned transplant. I can still recall, all these years later, her doctor's voice and manner as he told me the medical team felt helpless and deflated. The new heart just did not fit.

Fitting in at work obviously doesn't have such dramatic life-or-death consequences in the physical sense, but I can attest that organ rejection in companies occurs more often than we probably think, and it leaves in its wake a *different* kind of death—that of one's hopes and dreams. Throughout my career, I have seen executive women leave organizations more often because they did not fit with the leadership team, or rather, the leadership team could not get comfortable with them than because they lacked the requisite skills. You could always tell when "fit" was the issue because the public announcement usually went something like this: "She is leaving to spend more time with her teenage children."

I have children. They are young adults now, but of course, for several years they were teenagers. And even as much as I love my girls, I feel pretty confident saying that I know very few executive women who would leave a great job at a high level (one that they have worked their entire adult life to get) so that they can "spend more time" with their teenage children! It is just a highly unlikely scenario.

For that matter, I have not met many teenagers who *wanted* their mothers to stay home so they could spend more time with them. It is just a logical disconnect. The ability to fit in (or not fit in, whichever the case may be) has gradually become the catch-all term for the myriad reasons a company's leaders decide an executive is no longer welcome. Perhaps the executive lost his or her champion. Perhaps the company was just not ready for the "transplant" they thought they needed. Perhaps the departing executive had bitten off more than he or she could chew. The list of possibilities is endless. But what is certain is that fit absolutely matters, one way or another. No, it doesn't mean that everyone must strictly conform to the same cookie-cutter standards and fixed formulas, but it *does* mean that an effort should be made, at least somewhat, to adhere to a majority standard while still being your authentic self—which does not bode well for people who are not the majority.

> I am the Black woman who joined the company of mostly all White men; or I'm the fashionista that goes to work in bright colors only to sit among people in boring gray, blue, black, and (ugh) brown. I once had a smart, competent young woman tell me that she never wore heels to work until I started at the company. She figured that if I could do it at my level, it must be okay.

Whether on purpose or not, I stand out. I am the Black woman who joined the company of mostly all White men; or I'm the fashionista that goes to work in bright colors only to sit among people in boring gray, blue, black, and (ugh) brown. I once had a smart, competent young woman tell me that she never wore heels to work until I started at the company. She figured that if I could do it at my level, it must be okay. But it isn't just attire that makes me stand out. I am the one who speaks up with unique perspectives only to be met with blank stares. I am the colleague that people have described as an "acquired taste"—yes, this has happened. I am the colleague that people bet on how long I will last at the company.

I have been counseled to try to "fit in more" and told to work harder to get along with so-and-so (although I am confident that that individual was not receiving the same counsel). Sometimes that meant holding my tongue when I normally would not. Sometimes it has meant conflicting counsel from colleagues and superiors on who and how I should be. Should I change the way I dress? Alter the way I look? Wear less jewelry and more muted colors? Be nicer? Be not as nice? Stop trying to be perfect? Make sure everything goes well and recognize that there is no room for error? Be direct? Be less direct? It felt like a constant balancing act.

I have been advised to leave a company by "well-meaning" colleagues. I have been told I would never be allowed to be successful at certain companies. I have even been told that I would never be taken seriously because I looked like a Barbie doll. *It is exhausting.*

Still, if you are in a work situation that feels like an ill-fitting suit, I think it is worth leaving room for the possibility that things can turn around. You may just need a settling-in period. My mother's first organ donor was a young man in his twenties, and his heart fit, at least at first. Just like my mother's doctors tried every intervention to ensure that the new heart fit, I believe those of us who do not naturally fit into an organization should exert that same level of effort. *Try* to make it fit. Put in the work. You owe it to yourself. And we owe it to those who will come after us.

In most instances, it is better to stay and drive change than leave without making an impact. But when you know for sure that your heart simply does not fit, leave before it stops beating. Leave before death occurs. Because, just as I saw with my mother, rarely can the new heart withstand the trauma. Do not wait for the organ rejection.

Not too long ago I attended a diversity seminar, and a woman who was the keynote speaker was fabulously *different*. She was everything the company I was working for would have rejected. She would have been organ rejection on steroids. Corporate roadkill. But she owned her uniqueness and fierce authenticity, and she embraced it in such a beautiful way that it left me in awe. She had a lot to say that morning, and she ended her presentation with words that I will never forget. Today, I still deeply believe in their essential truth. She said, in a nutshell: "I'm tired of trying to cram my sparkly, star-shaped self into society's beige, square holes. I choose to embrace my ridiculous awesomeness and shine like the freaking supernova I was meant to be." It was (and still is) oddly empowering.

Since I started this chapter with a quote by Dr. Seuss, I think it only fitting that I make my point by ending with him. Though Dr. Seuss focuses his stories on children, a closer look reveals that there is almost always a deeper, more expansive message being delivered to adults—and *The Sneetches* is no different.

In the story, there are two kinds of bird-like pot-bellied creatures called Sneetches, which are distinguished by having or not having stars on their bellies. The Star-Belly Sneetches think they are the best, and they look down upon the Sneetches without stars. The Plain-Belly Sneetches are depressed and oppressed and prohibited from associating with their star-bellied counterparts until Sylvester McMonkey McBean comes along with his *Star-on* and *Star-off* Machine. He begins to give stars to the Plain-Belly Sneetches, and soon they are happy, for they look like their "elite" counterparts. The original Star-Belly Sneetches, of course, are angry at no longer being different and special, so they get

My maternal great grandmother, Fannie Harper King, and great grandfather, Reverend William King.

My mother, Dorthy Lockhart, at sixteen years old.

My childhood home in Oakland, California.

In the backyard with my mother when we lived in Albuquerque, New Mexico.

My school picture when I was around ten years old.

Me and my friend
Dennis at Texas Tech
University, where we were
cheerleading partners
(around 1983).

One of my favorite
photos taken when I
was on the field as a
cheerleader for the
Washington Redskins
NFL team, now known
as the Washington
Football Team. This
was taken in 1989.

Our wedding day. Greg and I were married on Memorial Day, May 27, 1991.

Me with my mother at my wedding. She was still recovering from her first heart transplant, which had been performed just a few months earlier.

May 1994, graduation from American University with an MA in Public Communication. Our first daughter was born two months earlier.

Our family of four. Savannah (left, on rocking horse), age 2, Jené, age 4. Charlene and Greg

July 8, 2017. Greg shaved my head that morning because it started falling out in clumps due to the chemotherapy treatments I started a month earlier.

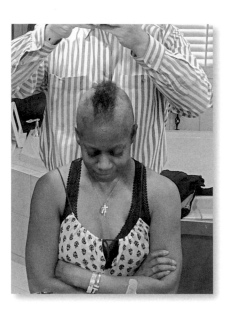

The last day of chemotherapy infusion. The sign was made by coworkers. August 10, 2017

My family at the Breast
Cancer Walk in Washington,
D.C. in September 2017.

My way of saying "thank
you" to the Charlie's
Angels team at the
Breast Cancer Walk.

Greg and me at our Vow
Renewal dinner after the
ceremony on September
10, 2018, in Bora Bora.

Hanging out at the office one day in the fall of 2019. Photo courtesy of Heather Philbin Photography.

Savannah, Greg, me, and Jené (2016).

Me and our dogs Chivas (left) and Remy (right). Photo courtesy of Heather Philbin Photography (2020).

Sylvester to remove all their stars. This continues back and forth until no one can remember which Sneetches originally had stars. This confusion creates a sudden epiphany: it really does not matter whether you have a star on your belly or not! We are all the same. So, thank you, Dr. Seuss, for your wisdom-at-any-age life lesson:

> "That day, all the Sneetches forgot about stars
> And whether they had one, or not, upon thars."

So, fit in, yes. But also remember to be courageous enough to shine as brightly as you please.

CHAPTER EIGHT

WORK IS PERSONAL

> **❝** Nobody cares how much you know
> until they know how much you care."
> THEODORE ROOSEVELT

We have all heard it before, probably many times throughout the years: "It's not personal; it's business." Usually, we hear these words or say them in connection with negative or so-called constructive feedback. Fully acknowledging that I have used this approach more than once, I have come to believe, over time, that it is the coward's way out of delivering a less-than-positive message. It helps people rationalize the negative news they are about to impart. Now that I have evolved, I find the whole concept of work not being personal insulting. Here is the bottom line: work *is* personal. Whenever there are people involved, it is personal. Period.

"It's not personal, it's business" is the corporate equivalent of a personal breakup that starts with "It's not you, it's me." The fact of the matter is that it *is* you, if not entirely, then partly. If you were not part of the problem, there would not be a need for a breakup! So, let us just agree now that work is personal, and we, as leaders, managers, and coworkers need to remember this message and lead with feeling.

I had a tough time with this concept early- to mid-career. I have always worked at companies where people say, "We're like family." Every time I hear that, I say to myself, "No—this is a *job*. I did not come to work to gain another family. I already have one waiting for me at home." Early in my career, I would even express my view aloud but quickly realized that my honesty was not appreciated, so I went underground with my thoughts. Meaning, I kept them to myself.

I used a similar "people-driven" concept to launch this chapter with the quote from Teddy Roosevelt, who reminds us that people really don't care about how smart you are or what you know until they see how much you care. It took me years to learn this lesson. I started my career during the days when people went to great lengths to separate their personal and business lives. I did it, too—with a vengeance—almost never divulging information about my personal life to colleagues. I did not know it at the time, but this approach did not do me any favors. In fact, it probably hurt me a bit because it permitted people to develop perceptions of me that were often incorrect and even unkind. A fellow executive once told me that I should tell people about my background more often because people would like me more. I had no idea what to do with that piece of information . . . though I certainly understand it now.

The first time I was faced with this conflict as a leader, it was perplexing to me. When I started in that executive position, it was clear to me the staff was at least 50 percent larger than necessary for the size of the business. Within the first thirty days (or so) of being in my new position,

I laid off *nearly half my staff*. People were pissed, even the employees who still had a job. While I was feeling proud of myself for having saved the company a significant amount of money, employees were running to Human Resources (and any other managers who would listen) to complain and share with them what an awful person I was. They denounced my actions. They said I did not care that I had just put so many people out of work and had made a rash decision. They said I was clearly the wrong person for the job.

I did not get it. Honestly, I did not. Beforehand, I told my staff the plan and worked with my leadership team to identify the positions that were redundant or unnecessary. I held all-hands meetings, I wrote communications, and *still* people expressed shock and anger. I would love to tell you that people eventually came around, but they did not. I only worked there for two years, and it was one of the best jobs I ever had because I learned a lot of leadership lessons, and I learned them the hard way. It was also the worst job I ever had because it was the first time I worked with people who blatantly hated me. In my mind, I was hired to do a job, not make new friends, so I was not going to be deterred; the work was too important.

> Looking back, I realize that even though the team performed well, what I did not allow room for was the exploration of their potential— the exploration of how great our team *could have* been. It was the missed opportunity for the team.

Although I learned my lesson and things eventually turned out fine, I would rather have my fingernails pulled out than go through that experience again. From a professional perspective, I did not make any of my decisions based on the people themselves, just on their jobs. And still, we performed some of the best work of my career. Looking back, I realize that even though the team performed well, what I did not allow room for was the exploration of their potential—the exploration of how great our team *could have* been. It was the missed opportunity for the team. Do not get me wrong: I was not completely cold, and I have always cared about people, but work was work.

Several years later, I joined another company that, again, had a staff larger than was probably necessary. I now had experience, though, so I had no intention of laying off *anyone* until it was truly clear it was unavoidable. At first, the team was excited for me to be there. They had been wanting a leader with my skillset for quite a while. I developed a strategy for the company and the team, put people in groups to execute that strategy, and hired consultants to help each team in case they felt like fish out of water. It was great—until I looked up about six months later and realized we had made little-to-no progress. Zilch.

A few weeks later, at church, my pastor quoted Teddy Roosevelt (the words used at the beginning of this chapter). Then, I came across Dr. Maya Angelou's quote that is similar: "I've learned that people will forget what you said, people will forget what you did, but people will never forget how you made them feel." A light bulb went off, and it hit me: my team was not making progress because, among other things, I had not taken the time to authentically connect with them on a personal or professional level. To them, I was all about me and my success, not them and their success. So, I began to show a more personal side of myself, slowly but surely. Now *I* was the fish out of water.

My husband and I host a large summer party each year, and my boss suggested I invite my team. I thought to myself, "Why would I do that? Why would I want to share my personal life for people to judge?" Now, I love to have parties, but I have host-phobia big time. I always worry that no one is going to show. It is completely irrational, of course, but then fears usually are. I didn't want to share that potential humiliation with the people who worked on my team.

I did invite the team. Not all, but most, of them came, though I am sure they felt like they *had* to come; I mean, when your boss invites you to something, you feel obligated. I was nervous about the whole thing, of course, but we ended up having a great time, and it completely changed our relationships for the better from that moment on. I was reminded of a book I had read by Marshall Goldsmith, *What Got You Here Won't Get You There*. The title says it all, and I learned the lesson. To this very day, I still hold many of those people who were part of that team in high regard, and I would do nearly anything to help them be successful.

I saw the true meaning of Dr. Angelou's quote, though, when I told the team that I had breast cancer and would be out of the office for several months. They were not concerned about the work; they were concerned about *me*. They rallied in a way I could have never imagined. They showered me with meaningful gifts, they researched the items that would bring comfort to people going through breast cancer treatment, and they made sure I had plenty of those items on hand. They made "open when" cards to keep my spirits up, which are cards that you open when you are feeling a certain way (the envelope will say "open when you need encouragement" or "open when you need a laugh," etc.). They came to visit, they made a book of handwritten letters for my birthday, and they protected my privacy. And in one of the

> I could not believe that the team and so many others came together to raise money in my honor. Firsthand, I saw and experienced the rewards of remembering—and embracing the fact—that business *is* personal. It just is.

greatest shows of support, they put together a team to walk in a breast cancer fundraiser (which I describe in the blog post included in this chapter). I could not believe that the team and so many others came together to raise money in my honor. Firsthand, I saw and experienced the rewards of remembering—and embracing the fact—that business *is* personal. It just is.

Had I not changed, had I not made the decision to share more of my personal side and focus on how I made people feel as a leader, I would have missed out on all the care and compassion I received from the team. I have thought more than once that cancer gave me the gift of knowing that I had impacted people's lives, and they mine. I believe our legacies are not about what we build or what we have started, but rather it is in the lives we touch along the way.

When the walk ended and the crowd dispersed, I went home and later wrote what I consider to be one of my most meaningful blog posts. I have said thank you to that team so many times, but it does not come close to fully expressing the deep appreciation I have for them. I have heard this said often, and you probably have, too, that the only time you are in a place where you hear so many nice things about someone is at their funeral, but by then it is too late. That day was, and remains, one of the best days of my life. Sometimes when you are feeling your weakest, others step in and become the strength you need.

I hope you enjoy this blog post as much as I enjoyed writing it.

◆ ◆ ◆

Why Me?

There are times in your life when something negative but meaningful happens to you. If you are like me, you never ask, "Why me?" because the truth is, "Why not me?" That is how I felt when I was diagnosed with breast cancer in February. Since then, I have been on an amazing journey filled with many inconveniences, pain, and dark days. But it takes rain to make rainbows, and yesterday a rainbow shone so brightly in my life I am still blinded by its presence. Yesterday was the Susan G. Komen Race for the Cure. My coworkers put together a team called Charlie's Angels, based on my nickname, Charlie. It was overwhelming to see so many people there to support women and men who have been affected by breast cancer. And a team put together to support me. I know I am not the only reason people on the Charlie's Angels team walked, but I know the idea started with Amy and Dawn, and a few others, out of concern for me. I am so humbled and so blessed—more than I can appropriately put into words. Charlie's Angels raised $24,000 in just over a month! These are some amazing people. I will never be able to thank them and others enough for the outpouring of love, concern, and action. And even from people I do not know. My family, friends, and even acquaintances have taught me so much about love, kindness, selflessness, and what it really means to be a blessing to others.

Cancer changes you physically, emotionally, and mentally. I look at pictures of myself before I was diagnosed and think that I will never again be that carefree person. I mourn who I was and question who I am becoming.

I look in the mirror and feel sad for the person looking back at me. It is a harrowing feeling.

Then I tell my reflection to "put on her Big Girl Pants and get through this." And that once this is done, I know I owe it to others to help them see that there is life on the other side. Even though my journey is not over, my will is stronger than ever because of Charlie's Angels, because of my family and friends, and because of God, who has taken me down this path for reasons I may never know. But I trust. I trust that in time it will all be okay. In time I will know how to express my gratitude.

In the meantime, I will excerpt the great poet E.E. Cummings, to express how I feel about so many who have touched my life:

i carry your heart(i carry it in my heart)

CHAPTER NINE

NOT EVERYONE IS INVESTED IN YOUR SUCCESS

" Injustice anywhere is a threat
to justice everywhere."
DR. MARTIN LUTHER KING JR.

Understand this:

Not everyone is invested in your success; some people are actively invested in your *failure*.

You will never win them over.

It is not about you; it is about them.

Realize this early and move on.

While I feel strongly about all the lessons in this book, this one digs deep for me because it is the one that has hurt me the most throughout my career. There is a lot of pain I understand, but I do not understand betrayal. And while I do not expect people to just stand blindly in my corner, I do not expect them to actively work against me, either—and, in many cases, actually *enjoy* it. Someone told me a long time ago that you can be successful and have enemies, or you can be unsuccessful and have friends. I did not pay it much attention at the time. In fact, I thought it was a rather cynical and a harsh way to the view the world. Until I did not. Until I learned the hard way. Until I realized, from seeing it unfold in my *own* life, that not everyone is going to be invested (or even interested) in my success, and, yes, there will be people who will actively work toward ensuring my failure. Sure, I've worked with people who frustrated me and who made me question their competence, but it never occurred to me to develop and execute a plot to ensure they would fail. I mean, who has that much time? A lot of people do. We all know that bullying happens. We all know that some people are simply self-centered jerks. But I never stopped to think that just because these bullies and blowhards become adults doesn't mean that they've actually grown up. Did you know that there is an organization called the Workplace Bullying Institute? (I didn't either, but more on that later.)

There were times in my career when it was clear that I was successfully climbing the corporate ladder one rung at a time. I was succeeding in defying the odds and overcoming unflattering stereotypes. I was shattering ceilings, busting up biases, and receiving loads of positive feedback from executives and leaders who were well-placed in the various organizations at which I worked. To say I was full of myself is an overstatement, but I felt good about myself and was proud of my accomplishments. Yes, I was definitely the "it" girl, and that felt good, too; I'll admit it. (Who *doesn't* want to be the "it" girl or guy at one time or another?) In some cases, I was used as an example of how to succeed and meld within a company culture quickly. I was on my way, and I had plenty of people who were cheering me on and rooting for me. *Wow,* I would think to myself. *Not bad for a little Black girl from Sobrante Park.* I was clearly the star of my own show.

But stars also fall. There is one tactical mistake I made again and again while my star was climbing. During my ascent, I failed to notice the people lurking in the corners, figuratively speaking, and sometimes people hiding in plain sight who were anything but "Team Charlene." These were the people playing offense, wanting to win their own game at any cost, just waiting for me to fail. They were what business books and articles often refer to as *saboteurs.* In the spirit of "keep your friends close and your enemies closer," I was confident that I could win them over. I'd reach out to them to befriend them, I would confide in them to help build trust, and, if I supervised them, I would give them opportunities for visibility and credibility with leadership so they could shine, too. And almost every time, my good intentions and actions came back to bite me in the ass—hard. Hard enough to make me regret it, but not so hard that I stopped believing in the inherent goodness in people. Instead of getting mad, I would seriously try to figure out how I could help them. But most of the time, that was not what they wanted, not what they were looking for, and not what they cared about. The plain and simple truth of the matter is this: *there was something about me and my success that got under their skin.* I decided that the adage was true: haters do not really hate you; they hate themselves, and your only mistake is to embody what they wish they could be. But knowing this essential truth didn't make it any easier.

On one occasion I decided to give more autonomy to a large group of competent professionals who worked for me and purposefully gave them more room to do their best work without me being in the way. Sure, they reveled in the independence—but they also used their access to leadership to besmirch and betray me, telling made-up stories about how I behaved or when I arrived at work (okay, so I *am* chronically late), or implying that I didn't do any work and just assigned it all to my team. (I am confident that had I been more of a micromanager, they would have complained about that, too: I hovered and got involved too much, created an atmosphere of insecurity and distrust, or did not give them the professional room to grow. The list could go on and on.) It was, without a doubt, a no-win situation. They would come up with *anything*, including half-truths, whole lies, implausible mischaracterizations that would turn my supporters and the leadership against me, or at least give them a reason to doubt me. That is the thing when you are in the minority or different: not only are you working against misconceptions, you are also fighting what is often referred to as *negative confirmation bias*, which is the need people have to see things in a certain way so that it confirms their own negative views and validates their own prejudices. You see this in politics all the time.

And almost every time, my good intentions and actions came back to bite me in the ass—hard. Hard enough to make me regret it, but not so hard that I stopped believing in the inherent goodness in people.

I remember another specific case. There was the boss I inherited who just did not like me. At every turn, she tried to discredit me on anything she could think of (my work, my inability to develop relationships, her perception of my lack of intelligence) and, unfortunately, most of the time she was successful. She held more influence than I did, and she was smart enough to choose when, where, and how to attack. There was not enough room at that company for both of us.

There were also times when women used my personal activities against me. Around the same time I started my career, I was also an NFL cheerleader. Many men, not surprisingly, found this tidbit about my background interesting (and even alluring, I think). Women, not so much. For some women, this was just more ammunition and further justification, in their minds, for not taking me seriously. They would say things like, "How smart can she *be*? She's a cheerleader, after all!" which only demonstrated how negative confirmation bias can seep in and poison the well. As for me, I purposely put my children in cheerleading and dance because I know that it teaches leadership, collaboration, how to lose gracefully, how to support others who are better than you, and how to win and lose as a team.

A sad but common observation: many people believe that the biggest saboteurs of women are other women. An article in the *Wall Street Journal* put it rather succinctly, saying, "Women who achieved success in male-dominated environments were at times likely to oppose the rise of other women. This occurred, [researchers] argued, largely because the patriarchal culture of work encouraged the few women who rose to the top to become obsessed with maintaining their authority." Personally, I think the tide is shifting on that belief, but only time and experience will tell.

I once took over a position that was previously held by a man (come to think of it, that's happened throughout my entire career!), but in this instance, he felt that my appointment was a poor reflection on *him*. As though by succeeding him, the leadership was saying that just about anybody could do that job. He refused to really acknowledge me as the new leader. In meetings he would be dismissive, passive-aggressive in his comments, and openly questioning of my decisions and judgment in front of others.

Another instance involves someone lodging an official complaint that I was careless with the company's money when I was on business trips. That led to an intense internal audit of me. In the end, I was cleared, and it was clear that the issue was with the other person, but some of the stink still rubbed off on me. I remember wondering, "Why me? What did I ever do to her?" Not a damn thing, really. But in her mind, I had snubbed her, and she fired back.

Perhaps the most surprising and most hurtful time was when a couple of male colleagues determined that I was in a weakened state due to illness, and they chose to use my weakness against me. I swear it was like sharks tasting blood. They proved, at least to me, that a well-placed male enemy with deep connections in the old boys' network can't be ignored and must be taken very seriously. One backroom political maneuver by a male rival can erase what you have earned with your hard work and grit.

It reminds me of elements of Black history, of how Blacks have been begrudged for achieving any kind of success post-slavery and resented for showing confidence and self-assurance, referred to as "uppity Blacks" (except the "n-word" would have been used instead). I am not saying that is what happened in my case, but I am saying that is how it *felt*. Like there was an undercurrent that Blacks needed to "know their place." Somehow, my success as a woman of color was a personal affront to these misguided souls with their misguided perceptions.

Although most of these personal examples above involve women, women have not been the biggest antagonists in my career. I have found myself attacked or made to feel small more often by men than women. In this, I am an anomaly. Research published in *The Journal of Development and Learning in Organisations* found that 70 percent of female executives feel as though they have been bullied by other women in their workplaces and that these bullying incidents have stunted their professional growth. You've heard of this before: It's often referred to as "The Queen Bee Syndrome." A Queen Bee in a workplace situation is a high-ranking woman in a position of authority who treats women who work below her more critically than their male counterparts. The Workplace Bullying Institute (I promised I'd get back to this!) reports even more startling findings, saying that women bully other women about *80 percent of the time.*

Further, recently, *Forbes* magazine reported that women who report to women experience a greater frequency of bullying, abuse, and job sabotage: "Women have fought and continue to fight for a seat at the table and to be seen as equal to their male counterparts. However, this fight often comes with challenges of its own." Author Marilyn Devonish, a certified neurolinguistic programming trainer, says the women who rise to the top "often take on a more aggressive leadership style in order to fit in and thrive." This is often referred to as *toxic masculinity* because women model the behavior of their successful male peers and make it a part of their own leadership style. *Ladies, we can do better.* And, fortunately, through efforts like #MeToo and *LeanIn.org*, things are beginning to change for the better.

Learning this led me to think again about my own behavior on occasion. Although I often saw myself as a victim, was I also a villain? My answer: Yes, I know there were times when I was unnecessarily harsh with my team members and pushed females harder than the males on the team. I recall one time being on the phone with a female coworker until late into the night, insisting she continue working on a report until we got it right. To this day, she will tell you that she hated me for that, but she gives me credit for working with her until it was done. We were both up into the wee hours of the night, working the project together. Nonetheless, as an overachiever, it took me a while to learn that I couldn't push everyone as hard or as long as I wanted. Some people aren't looking to

Author Marilyn Devonish, a certified neurolinguistic programming trainer, says the women who rise to the top "often take on a more aggressive leadership style in order to fit in and thrive." This is often referred to as toxic masculinity because women model the behavior of their successful male peers and make it a part of their own leadership style. Ladies, we can do better.

prove anything; they just want a nine-to-five job. I nearly fired a woman for this once. Her desire to have a regular job appeared to me to be a lack of commitment to the company. I was wrong in how I treated her, and yes, I was probably a bully. When I see people who are talented beyond what they can see, I have a tendency to be hard on them to help them reach their potential. In most cases it works out, but it doesn't mean I did not make them feel bullied at one time or another.

At first, I did not believe that people who knew me, or even just knew of me, would engage in any type of corporate sabotage against me. I mean, why? What was in it for them? Are some adults really that insecure that they gain satisfaction from someone else's misfortune? So frightened about their own futures that they need to tear others down to build themselves up? It was like being in high school all over again, where you had your popular people, your jocks, your nerds, your stoners, and, yep, your bullies. I could not easily accept that in a workplace of adults people would spread rumors, tell lies, or tear people down just because they could. It didn't compute.

One Sunday at church, my pastor was preaching about people living beyond their means just to prove things that don't really matter or to seem worthy in someone else's eyes. He said something to the effect of, "We buy things we don't need with money we don't have to impress people we don't like." I've heard similar quotes from other people. Another of my favorite pastors, Joel Osteen, brought the point home best (and here, I'm paraphrasing): When you live in a proving mode, it's like you're on a treadmill. As soon as you prove to one person that you are okay, you will see somebody else you need to impress. You are working hard but not going anywhere. Get off that treadmill—you have to accept that some people, no matter what you do, are not going to like you. No matter how nice you are, they are not going to approve of you. You have to be at peace with people not being at peace with you.

Can I get an Amen?

I accepted that there will always be people who are not on my side, and there will always be people who will actively try to derail me. The positive flip side of this troubling knowledge is that there will also be people who are there to help me. It is important to remember that. Focus on the positive. Those who want to help will outnumber those who do not.

How do you know if you are being sabotaged at work? If it's obvious, you can deal with it: A colleague consistently withholds critical information, shoots down your ideas in meetings, starts rumors about you, refuses to pitch in to help, refuses to offer helpful advice, tries to make you look bad in front of the boss, forgets to invite you to that big project meeting— you know the drill. But the tell-tale sign that the damage has been inflicted is when people start to treat you differently. The shift might be gradual or sudden, but when it begins to happen (and it will if you're not careful), *this* is cause for real concern.

And that is when I accepted that there will always be people who are not on my side, and there will always be people who will actively try to derail me. The positive flip side of this troubling knowledge is that there will also be people who are there to help me. It is important to remember that. Focus on the positive. Those who want to help will outnumber those who do not.

So, is your only option to just grin and bear it? Hell no. But women do need to be cautious about how they address some of the Machiavellian behaviors that can unfold in the workplace. How you respond can either improve or exacerbate the situation. In my situation at work with the disloyal colleagues, once I truly recognized what was going on, I went into full fight-or-flight mode. I fought back, which is the right thing to do some of the time. I confronted the accuser and sometimes went to the boss about it. And you know what? More often than not, I was the one who ended up looking sophomoric, whiny, and unprofessional. They call it a "boys' club" for a reason.

Therefore, when faced with these situations now, the first place I start is with myself, by looking inward and seeing if I was in any way the catalyst for this behavior. After all, in all those situations, the common denominator was me. And that is what makes corporate bullying so insidious: something is done to hurt you, yet you have or might have convinced yourself it was somehow your fault. I learned my lesson, I suppose. I now know not to get angry, at least not outwardly. Who wants to be the bitter Black woman in the office? Besides, bitterness, anger, and resentment often lead to self-sabotaging and irrational behavior. I have learned to not let my suspicions turn to paranoia. And, I have learned to be the bigger person. You must master these skills, too.

To borrow from former First Lady Michelle Obama, "When they go low, we go high." We have no other choice, really—not one that will work in our favor, anyway. I think the best we can do is to continue doing our jobs, build strong relationships and our personal brands as best we can to generate good will and earn the benefit of the doubt, keep our eyes open, and, most importantly, ignore the haters. Just don't forget that they are there. Chances are, you are spending a lot more time thinking about them than they are thinking about you.

One of my dear friends from college, Dennis, used to say to me, "Don't let him live in your head rent-free!" (I was usually obsessing about an unrequited love.) I don't think I really understood the saying back then, but I certainly do now. What he meant was that I should not spend any time thinking about someone who did not care about me. Let's face it: some people just are not going to like you. Recognize it early, keep an eye out, and *move on*. Do not let saboteurs make you self-sabotage. When this happens, they win.

A few years ago, Linda Smith, CEO of The Meanest Woman Alive, LLC, wrote an article in *Entrepreneur* magazine, "How to Protect Your Career from Those Who Try to Undermine You." In it, she wrote:

> The sad truth is that women in business must always be on the lookout for people who will try to discredit them. The opposition could come in the form of a direct challenge to your authority or a sneak attack to damage your reputation with your clients, your customers, your bosses, and peers. Ask any woman in any line of work, and she'll tell you how simple it is for a carefully planted seed of doubt or a well-placed bit of gossip to jeopardize her position by raising questions about her professional competence or her effectiveness in her business. Watching your back, unfortunately, is an inescapable part of the track to success."

Pretty depressing. I am competitive, sure—but never at someone else's expense. So, I was ill-prepared when I figured out that the same person who could smile in your face could be the same person stabbing you in the back. For years (and still today), my email signature quotes Abraham Maslow, the groundbreaking psychologist and creator of Maslow's Hierarchy of Needs: "Assume Good Will." Sabotage or not, that is just how I choose to approach the people in my life: assume that they are well intentioned (at least until I find out they are not).

My exercise instructor always says, "Follow your heart *and* your gut, for they will never lead you astray."

And if that does not work, follow the eloquent words of the late, great Elizabeth Taylor: "Pour yourself a drink, put on some lipstick, and pull yourself together."

I want to close this chapter by sharing a parable. And while I haven't been able to confirm the author, I include it here because it reminds us that regardless of the challenges women and minorities experience in the workplace, one of the most effective antidotes is *knowing our value and being true to it*. I've seen several versions, but this is the one I like best.

Before she died, a mother said to her daughter, "Here is a watch that your grandfather gave me. It is almost two hundred years old. Before I give it to you, go to the jewelry store downtown. Tell them that I want to sell it, and see how much they offer you." The daughter went to the jewelry store, came back to her mother, and said, "They offered a hundred and fifty dollars because it's so old." The mother then said, "Go to the pawn shop." The daughter went to the pawn shop, came back to her mother, and said, "The pawn shop offered ten dollars because it looks so worn." The mother asked her daughter to go to the museum and show them the watch. She went to the museum, came back, and said to her mother; "The curator offered half a million dollars for this very rare piece to be included in their precious antique collections." The mother said, "I wanted to let you know that the right place values you in the right way. Do not find yourself in the wrong place and get angry if you are not valued. Those that know your value are those who appreciate you; don't stay in a place where nobody sees your value."

Recognize your value. Know your worth. And whenever possible, assume good will.

CHAPTER TEN

IT IS NOT ALL ABOUT YOU

 Life's most persistent and urgent question is, 'What are you doing for others?'"

DR. MARTIN LUTHER KING JR.

Most of us did not get to where we are today on our own. Our accomplishments mean little if we do not reach out and help those who will come after us. Not just in work, but in life. And herein is another important lesson: *It is not all about you.*

Sitting in my office one morning, a colleague, a woman of color, tapped on my door to ask if I had a few minutes to talk. I was a little surprised since I'd only been at the company for a couple of weeks, and I'd only introduced myself to her that very morning. I could not imagine what problem she might have that would lead her to seek advice from me so early in the game. I directed her to my conference table. After the exchange of typical pleasantries, she told me that she stopped by to tell me that she was happy that I had been hired into the company, and that, to her knowledge, I was the first Black female executive ever at the company. Although the company had existed for more than fifty years, she was right: I *was* its first Black female corporate executive.

She told me that she hoped I would stay with the company. She talked about how she and her friends at work did not think it was possible for a Black woman to be an executive there or to move up through the ranks, but that I was evidence that it was indeed possible. I could feel her sense of relief and see it on her face. To her, my presence represented hope for her and other Black women. It meant that the company was aligning its words with its actions regarding diversity. Although I was the first, to her it meant that there could be—would be—another, and then another, and that there was now opportunity for her and her friends, where previously they saw none.

I thought about our conversation off and on for weeks, if not months. Over the span of my career in senior leadership positions, I have had this same (or a very similar) conversation with dozens of women and men. Mostly Black women, because what befalls Black women impacts *all* women, just in varying degrees. They all wanted pretty much the same thing from me: a listening ear, guidance, perspective, and reassurance that success was possible for them.

Although being the first and only was lonely, it has also been an honor and a tremendous source of personal and professional pride. But at some point, it also became a sort of burden. Would I change the positive things that happened in my career that led me to leadership? No, of course not. But I was keenly aware that my success was no longer only mine. It was the success-to-come of the women who saw me as a beacon of hope. Those women who would hopefully come after me. However, it also meant that my failures would be theirs as well. Maybe I took it all too personally, but I often felt like I was the test case, and my comfort-able corner office was the petri dish. If everything worked out, we would celebrate—but if it didn't, it was just further proof that a Black woman couldn't gain admittance to the private boys' club after all. The company could say they tried and then replace with me a middle-aged White man, which has happened many times.

In that job, things were hard. All the things that I have talked about in previous chapters were happening again and again, and I wanted out, at least some of the time. I am most always even keeled and calm—the picture of "grace under pressure," I have been told, even (perhaps *especially*) when things are crashing down around me. As I described in the last chapter, I rarely show outright anger, and it takes a lot for me to raise my voice to someone. I just do not do it. Unfortunately, because of this, people often perceived this to mean that I was aloof, I was intimidating, and I cared only about myself. If they only knew that, sometimes, at the end of the day, I'd be in tears driving my car out of the parking lot.

In fact, I cried on my commute home for about six months. Every day. And I do not mean those silent, pretty, polite tears. Sure, *sometimes* the tears were dainty and delicate, but other times it was just flat-out ugly crying. But true to form for me, as I approached my house, I would pull myself together and paste a smile on my face before I walked into the house so that no one was the wiser. I didn't want anyone to think that I couldn't handle it, not even my husband. I was embarrassed and felt helpless. It was a lonely time.

Throughout my career, like everyone I suppose, I got frustrated from time to time. The challenges, the biases—conscious and unconscious— and constantly being made to feel different, sometimes became too much. Occasionally, I thought it just was not worth it. There were times I felt I was banging my head against the wall, and I believed that the best thing for me to do was to call it quits. But I could not just quit. My throwing in the towel would have had wider-ranging implications. Wouldn't it represent a loss of hope for other women, and especially Black women? Or was I giving myself a little too much credit? Overestimating my own impact on others? I did not know. But what I *do* know is what it feels like to have hope—and the loss of that hope was something I was not willing to either accept or convey just because things got a little uncomfortable. I wanted to be the hope that some people needed. I wanted to ignite that same spark of hope in other women, too, but I couldn't do that if I wasn't there. This was about far more than just me.

While we women have every right to be proud of the success we have worked so hard to achieve, most of us did not get where we are today on our own. There were people along the way who helped, who propped us up when it was needed most. Our champions. I might not know every single soul whose shoulders I stood upon to be where I am today, but rest assured, I know they existed. I know they came before me. While we feel good about our individual and collective accomplishments, they mean little in the long run if we do not reach out and help those who will come after us. Just as we cannot take for granted those who came before us, neither can we forget to lift up those who wait in the wings. This is why you and I must support them, guide them, and prop them up. Because ladies (and men), it is not all about just us. It never has been, and it never will be.

When we reach the top rung on the ladder, we have a responsibility to reach back and pull up others. Do not be the woman who kicks others down the ladder once you make it to the top: extend the ladder or add another one and make room to elevate others, too. Be the woman who makes change happen. We are never more powerful than when we pull together. And we must do it deliberately, with a sense of purpose, passion, and commitment. Why? Because it is our collective responsibility. We belong to each other.

I have talked to countless women who have said that they were hesitant to reach out to other women. They were afraid that they might be labeled in a negative way and that maybe it was better for their career to focus on the men in power positions. They were not completely wrong. Research in *Academy Journal of Management* found that senior-level women who try to help other women at work are likely to face more negative performance reviews than those who do not. I totally get it—but I cannot accept it.

When I finished my cancer treatment and realized I was a bit lost and more than a bit depressed, I decided to start a blog, justbetweenusgirrls.com. I've already shared some of these blog posts in earlier chapters. I did not start writing this blog because I needed a personal outlet (I am quite comfortable internalizing everything, even if it is not good for me). As I've already mentioned, I started writing the blog because I did not want other women who were in the same situation as me to feel like they were alone. I wanted them to know that they were not going crazy, that they didn't need to isolate, and that, yes, there is help. I wanted the blog to take an honest, unapologetic, deep dive into the mental aspects of having cancer. I was lost and did not want others to feel lost, too. From the very outset, I promised to be honest and authentic, and I have kept that promise, even when it has been hard to do so. I cannot *not* be authentic.

When people who knew me personally started reading my blog, they were surprised by the sensitive topics I addressed, such as the insecurities that emerge because your body is no longer what it used to be and the concerns about whether your spouse will still find you attractive and still want to be with you; the concerns about your mortality and concern about all that you will leave behind; and your occasionally compromised intellectual capacity (because "chemo brain" is real). Some were shocked that I would be that open, that honest, that authentic. In a way, I shocked *myself*. Before cancer, I would never have been that transparent; I never would have revealed my weaknesses and vulnerabilities. *Never.* But cancer changes things. Today, I can honestly say I am more accepting of my own weaknesses and vulnerabilities as I am of my strengths. It all matters.

People asked me if I was concerned that all that honesty would reflect negatively on my professional life. They suggested that "oversharing" might not be good for my career. At first, I did not think about it at all. But then I started to think about it a lot. With each post, I became more concerned, and I started to doubt myself. I had spent thirty years building an extraordinary career; was I flushing it down the toilet by being weepy about having cancer? In the end, the answer was clear. I felt strongly that my purpose was much greater than my fear and that my passion was greater than my fear. This recognition was freeing in a way because I had discovered, or at least started to understand, why all of it was happening to me.

Yes, there are times when I am still very concerned, or I worry about what other people think or what they might be saying when I'm not around. Maybe it is positive, maybe it is not, but then again, maybe they are not talking about me at all—*it does not matter anymore.* I want to be authentically me, and I want to fully embrace everything that comes with it. Bring it on. My purpose is greater than my fear. And I guess I am asking the same of you, dear reader: let your purpose and your passion be greater than your fear at work and in life in general. Be intentional. Banish fear. Embrace your own authentic self. Own your beautiful self.

> My purpose is greater than my fear. And I guess I am asking the same of you, dear reader: let your purpose and your passion be greater than your fear at work and in life in general. Be intentional. Banish fear. Embrace your own authentic self. Own your beautiful self.

Whether in work or other situations, we can all identify areas that simply feel *wrong*, whether it is bias, harassment, inequity, whatever. Most of us will be able to identify it, and many more of us will say to ourselves or others, "Someone really needs to do something about that," or "When is someone going to see that this is wrong?" or "Why aren't they doing something?" It takes absolutely no effort whatsoever to ask the question, but it does not even matter that you ask the question *if you are not willing to do something about it yourself*. It is time. Time to figure out our purpose. Time to figure out what needs to change and then *change it*. Time to be passionate about making sure that change unfolds. Make it matter that you are here; our time on this Earth is finite. The days are long, but the years are short. Make them count. And when it comes to change and making change happen, I ask you, "If not you, then who?"

Reputations are built from what you accomplish. Legacies are made by the people whose lives you touch along the way. This next post, along with everything else in this book, is one way I am working to make change happen, to reach people and inspire them while I am passing through this one wonderful life.

◆ ◆ ◆

BLOG POST

Dragging My Feet

JANUARY 13, 2020

I have been writing this blog post for months—many months. I think my last post was in May last year. This is unusual for me. It generally takes me an hour to write a post, another hour to let it marinate, and then about thirty minutes to post it.

But this one has been harder. Different. I had planned to title it: "How Stella Got Her Groove Back" and share the many things I have learned over the past three years (yes, three years). The phrase is the title of a book and a movie written by the late Terry McMillan about a strong Black female (Stella) who comes back stronger after a setback. The title and post are a nod to me being "back" 100 percent. But the words just were not coming to me. When I started this blog, I committed to myself and my readers that I would always be authentic and transparent, even if it meant saying things that made me uncomfortable.

As I get better, it is harder to be transparent. To lay yourself bare for judgment. It is so much easier to build up walls. But I am not going to do that. So, that requires me to acknowledge that I am not 100 percent yet. I thought I was, but then I got sidelined. Not by my health, but by the health of others—people who I knew directly or through others who have not done so well. I know several people who have recently died from breast cancer, people who were considered survivors. It is sobering.

Late last year, I had an appointment with my surgeon in Texas. I was sure he would say I am done. He did not. I was told that one, maybe two, more surgeries are needed. As I walked out of the building, I felt sad. I wanted to cry. I wanted to ask God when this would be over or, at least, when will I have a day that does not include cancer. Rather than listening to my own whining, I looked up and looked out. I saw women who were bald, eyes sunken, some in wheelchairs and some not, but all just trying to make it through one more day. I realized that many of those women would prob-ably love to be where I am right now—over the hump of the worst treat-ments, able to walk on my own and work and do almost anything I want with less fear. I am blessed; I know that. Blessed beyond measure. I think it is no longer time for sadness. What is behind me was worse than what is ahead of me. It is time for some extreme optimism.

I now accept that I am not 100 percent. As I write this, I am in Houston at MD Anderson prepping for surgery on Tuesday. It is a lot. I have a lot to say to catch you up, but first, let me finish this post, which is my list to-date of how I am returning to myself, which are lessons I've learned along the way that just maybe will help you too.

1. **I forgive myself for getting cancer.** Intellectually, I know I did not cause my cancer, but deep down I think my lifestyle contributed to weakening my immune system. Did I work too much? Carry too much stress? Exercise too little? Internalize my concerns to the point it weakened my body and my immune system?

2. **I accept the "new" me, inside and out.** Recently, I went to see a cosmetic surgeon to have him look at something on my non-cancerous breast I did not like. He told me he could excise this and stitch that, etc. I told him I would think about it, but at this point, perfection is not the goal. Living is.

3. **I forgive others and approach most situations with empathy.** The thing about being sick is that it brings out the best and, sometimes, the worst in people. I mostly experienced the best ten times over. But I did see the other side, too. There were people who didn't know how to have a friend with cancer, so they didn't come around much; and there were people who knew how to take advantage of people in a weakened state—and did—for their gain. This hurts the most— the people who betray you because pushing you down helps them rise. To the former, I hold no grudge, no feeling of disappointment,

only understanding and a hope that we can reconnect. It can be hard having a sick friend. I get it. To the latter, those who took advantage of my weakened state, well, there is a special place in Hell for you.

4. **I have a responsibility to myself to choose how I channel my energy.** Where, how much, and when. I have said it before: time is finite. And I am thankful for every new day that I have.

5. **I discovered and tapped into things that bring me pure joy:** the perfect jalapeño margarita, cuddling with my dogs, driving my car with the top down and the wind in my hair, listening to music (Darius, of course), quiet moments with my husband, loud moments with my adult children as they regale me with stories of how they think they tricked us when they were kids (silly them) and their interesting lives now.

6. **I accept that disease is not fair.** I knew that life was not fair. Just like my grandmother told my mother decades ago, my mother taught me that life would not be fair for me as a Black female. So, I do not expect fairness in most situations. I really do not. But I thought disease affected all of us (broadly) in the same way. But then I learned that breast cancer death rates are 40 percent higher among Black women than White women. Is it because of lesser access to good healthcare? Maybe, but dozens of studies say it is much more than just that. Is there somewhere out there where the playing field is level for Black women? (The question is rhetorical).

7. **I do not know how to smoke pot** (is that still what it is called?). Someone gave me these bud-like things when I was going through chemo, but I did not know what to do with them. I Googled "how to smoke pot," and YouTube tried to show me the way. After twenty minutes of watching how-to videos, I decided it was easier to just take a nap. At least then, when I woke up, I did not have the munchies.

8. **I stopped wearing bras.** It is freeing. I have gorgeous bras adorned with crystals, rhinestones, lace, silk—you name it—but now they stay carefully arranged in several specially designed drawers that I never open because, frankly, these new breasts do not move.

9. **It matters that I am on this planet.** I have made a difference in some areas that really matter to me. I have a purpose. I know that now.

10. **And finally, I learned.** That is all. I learned. This list has only ten items, but I am sure I could come up with fifty more. Cancer taught me a lot in a relatively short period of time. There were some hard lessons. But I learned.

Coming full circle, Stella got her groove back, and I am pretty sure I will, too!

CHAPTER ELEVEN

THERE IS NO SUCH THING AS WORK-LIFE BALANCE

> " Have no fear of perfection.
> You'll never reach it anyway."
> SALVADOR DALI

It took me a long time to realize that "life lessons" are so named because it sometimes takes, quite literally, a *lifetime* to learn them. Here is another of those lessons that you simply cannot fully absorb until you've spent quite a bit of time—in some cases, a literal lifetime—experiencing it: *there is no such thing as a work-life balance.* Period. It does not (and should not) exist. Make your decisions about work and life, then own up to them. And do not beat yourself up about them—ever.

Every time I give a speech or presentation or moderate a panel, no matter the size of the crowd, I can count on being asked one question: "How do you achieve a work-life balance?" It's a fair question no matter where you are in your career. I find that early-career professionals often try carving out time for their personal lives, while mid-career professionals generally try to juggle what feels like a million things at once between raising children and cultivating a career, and many late-career professionals find themselves as empty-nesters searching for a way to fill the void. What do they fill it with? You guessed it: more work!

I am pleased to say that over the last five to six years, more young men ask that question than young women. Let's face it: people always have a lot to say about millennials (I have two myself, Jené and Savannah), and much of it is positive. But one thing is clear: unlike many of their more traditional fathers, many male millennials want to be home spending quality time with their kids, eating meals with them, playing with them, and putting them to bed. It seems the days of "Mom does everything at home and Dad has never changed a diaper in his life" are over. I applaud those young men. To them, I say, "Bravo!" because they are wanting to create a new balance and refusing to seek a balance in the old, traditional sense.

The question then becomes can you achieve work-life balance, especially with men more willing to pitch in? The answer is simple. No. Let me say it again: there is no such thing as the perfect work-life balance, so stop trying to find it, unless you just have a thing for expending fruitless effort and spinning your wheels needlessly. Instead, let me make these recommendations. I share them because they've worked for me; I share them from a place of truth: make your decisions about work and make your decisions about life, then own them. Do not apologize for them, and do not try to weave the separate threads into a single piece of fabric.

In my experience, if you are killing it at work and your boss is thrilled with your performance, I can pretty much guarantee you that your spouse and children don't feel the same way about how you're handling things at home. The opposite can be true, as well. If you've got the Mommy Thing down to a "T," if you're making sandwiches and cutting them into animal shapes to put in your kids' lunches, if you're home in time to help your kids with their homework, if you cook delicious, balanced dinners, put the kids to bed with a story, and serve your husband a nicely chilled glass of wine so that the two of you can sit down and discuss the day, then I guarantee you, you're probably close to being fired. Because you will *not* be killing it at work. It is just not possible to keep the two in balance at the same time. And it is not sustainable.

The next question, then, is "How do you make it work?" I usually say that I am working to have balance *in the aggregate*. By that, I mean a more holistic approach to balance; a more realistic approach to balance that respects its different territories. Not so much a balance, really, as a healthy respect for all the various commitments and responsibilities you have unfolding in your life at the same time. You're not trying to *balance* it all as much as you are trying to *own* it all by giving each its own, dedicated space.

I'm willing to bet that most of the working mothers who read this book will say that, at one time or another, they felt guilty or irresponsible about having (or wanting) to work instead of staying at home with their children. And most of the stay-at-home moms who read this book will probably admit that though they are glad they stayed home with their children, it would have been nice to have had some kind of career or job of their own. Nearly every mother at one time or another asks themselves if they made the right choice. Well, I am going to free you of your guilt right here and now, because *there is no one right choice*. The right choice is the one you make that works for you and your family.

Greg and I never spoke about having children before we got married. And once we were married, I was not dreaming of children, and he was not either, to my knowledge. This is a cautionary tale. Have that conversation, and you will save yourself a lot of anguish. Greg comes from a very traditional family. His father was a pastor, and his mother taught piano. Their family of seven ate dinner together every night, always at the same time. Visualize apron-clad June Cleaver handing her suit-wearing Ward his dinner plate while appreciating him for doing the "hard" work of going to the office. (If your memory won't take you that far back, perhaps a scene from *Mad Men* would resonate more authentically than my more dated *Leave It to Beaver* reference.) Neither of these scenes unfolded during my youth, however. I was raised by a single mother who often worked late or worked two jobs and was not home very often, so our approach to dinner was "every man for himself."

When Greg and I did have children, a lot of things surfaced we had never talked about before. Greg assumed he would go back to work and I would stay home and take care of the baby. I, on the other hand, assumed we would *both* go back to work and *someone else* (a nanny) would take care of the baby. Then, we had another baby, and all hell broke loose. Greg resented having to do most of the child-rearing work, and I resented him. Greg started talking about giving up one of our cars so we could afford for me to stay home. And with every word he said, I felt like the prison gates were closing in around me. I told him that if I gave up my career to be a stay-at-home mom *and* gave up my car, which represented independence to me, one day he would come home to an empty house. All my clothes would be gone, and there would be a note that said the kids are at the neighbors' and he would never see me again. I wasn't making a real threat, but I was trying to drive home an important point.

This had nothing to do with how much I loved my girls or my husband, of course. I would give my life for them. But it had everything to do with being independent and never being in the situation my mother was in for all those years of being married to an abusive husband simply because she had no other choice. I cannot overstate how important *choice* is to me. I would not have run away and left my children, of course, but you get my point. I have to know every day that I come home because I *want* to, not because I have no other choice. After years of marriage counseling and, as of this writing, twenty-nine years of marriage, we still have not completely resolved this issue. In the process, I've learned that "normal" families eat dinner together most nights. And he, like many other men, learned that when a man is with his children while his wife is out, it is not called babysitting, it is called *being with your children*.

For years, women have gotten the short end of the stick. While self-help books and magazines are telling us to focus on self-care, we are really just trying to get the right clothes on the right kid at the right time. I remember being in church on Sundays and seeing families with kids that were so smartly dressed—little girls in their Mary Janes and little boys in their neat, little bowties. Usually the father was dressed equally well. And then you'd look at the mother, who clearly just threw on something that she could find that was clean, smeared on some lipstick, and only combed the front of her hair because that's the part she could see. And I would think to myself that she should be more selfish. That was never going to be me, I promised myself.

I have a friend who also has two children, and she came to visit one day. I showed her how I had turned a bedroom into a custom closet. I opened a drawer that was designed specifically for buttons (you know, the extra buttons you get when you buy a jacket or a suit or dress). She looked in the drawer, saw how tidy it was, then burst into tears. She did not understand how I had the time to organize my buttons into their own, beautiful drawer when she was just hanging on by a very thin thread. I thought to myself and told her, "You should be more selfish."

Marriage counselors will tell you that the best thing you can do for your kids is love your spouse, and you should never put your children ahead of your spouse or even yourself. Clearly, these counselors are not familiar with the Mama Bear Syndrome, which means that we mothers will stop at nothing to protect our children. Even marriage counselors are telling us to be more selfish, but some of us just cannot get there. I do not seem to have that problem. Just ask my husband.

But it still begs the question: "If you cannot have work-life balance every day, how do you even get it in the *aggregate?*" Okay, here are my dirty little secrets. I guess I should describe these "secrets" as *solutions*, really, because that's precisely what they are. Listen up:

1. I outsource anything and everything that I can.

2. I do not apologize or even second-guess the decisions I have made so that my family situation works.

3. I let go of the guilt. It is a useless emotion.

4. I paid my daughter to not be a Brownie. (More on that later.)

5. I still have a nanny.

As you might imagine, since Greg and I didn't agree on who should stay home with the children (by the way, it was never a consideration for him to stay home), we pretty much couldn't agree on much else that involved the children or the house. Greg wanted to mow the lawn every Saturday morning. That is fine, but the guy who did my nails could only do them on Saturday morning. So, I would go get my nails done, and Greg would get exasperated because he then needed to take care of the girls, and evidently it was less comfortable to mow the lawn in the middle of the day during the summer. He once asked why it seemed every weekend I was getting something polished, painted, or buffed. Our solution was to hire a lawn service, even if that meant hiring a teenager down the street who needed extra money. Then, Greg realized that after he and the girls would play and mess up the house that I had just finished tidying, I would go into a crazy rage (which was always the silent treatment because I don't raise my voice), so we hired someone to come to the house every other week to help with cleaning. And so began the uber outsourcing.

When I realized how incredibly chaotic and difficult it was to get two toddlers dressed, fed, and to daycare and still get to work by nine, and how tired we both were of the pattern (especially him because I traveled a lot), we hired a nanny. This one was tough because that wasn't the kind of background I had, nor was it Greg's, but in order to maintain our sanity, we saw hiring a nanny as the solution. It was a big stretch money-wise for us, but we wanted to stay married, so it became a necessity. Never mind that my entire paycheck at the time went to pay for the nanny. (If you net it out, she probably made more than I did since she was an independent contractor.) *But it made things easier.* Both Greg and I are workaholics, and we were able to get to our comfort zones (work), come home and be with our girls (family), and ultimately make enough money to have a nanny *and* go out on occasion (our idea of a comfortable balance).

When my oldest daughter, Jené, was in fourth or fifth grade, she decided that she wanted to join the Brownies, the precursor group to the Girl Scouts. (I like Girl Scouts as much as the next person, especially during cookie season.) I spoke to the lead mother to make sure she understood that I supported Jené's decision, but that this could not be a mother-daughter thing because my schedule just did not accommodate it. We all agreed that was fine, so Jené started her Brownie career.

Within a couple of months, the lead mom called me to tell me that my daughter was the only little girl at the meetings who did not have a mother there. Hmm. Hadn't we *talked* about this already? Hadn't an agreement already been made at the very outset? I did not think they would accept me sending our nanny as a fill-in, so I promised my daughter and the lead mother that I would be at the next meeting. The day came, and at the appropriate time (well, really fifteen minutes *after* the appropriate time), I left the office and sped to school to pick up my daughter and take her to the meeting. The whole while, unfortunately, I had an earpiece in my ear, my phone in my hand, and I was finishing a business call as I walked into the room. And there they were. The Mommy Mafia. The perfect mothers, carefully coiffed, making perfect little crafts with their daughters, looking comfortable and mommy-appropriate in their sporty tracksuits and sensible shoes. There *I* was, on the other hand, in my business suit and high heels. Talk about a fish out of water.

Do you know how hard it is to crawl around a floor in a pencil skirt and a tailored jacket? When the meeting ended and my daughter and I were back in the car, she asked me if I could be sure to "dress like the other moms" the next time I came to another meeting. My heart broke into little pieces because her innocent request made its own powerful point: *I had embarrassed her.* There was no pride in having a working mommy, just disappointment that she didn't have a mommy like the other ones. I felt for her. But I still said no. I was sure I would never be a member of the Mommy Mafia. Now to be clear, I respect women who make the choice to stay home with their children. I hold those women who involve themselves in their children's extracurricular activities in the highest esteem. I know it's a hard job, and I begrudge them *nothing*. But I wasn't willing to trade in my business suit (i.e., my career) for a comfortable after-school ensemble (i.e., be in the permanent role of a stay-at-home mom). To those women who choose to, I salute you. All I'm saying is that it just wasn't me.

We got through that year, which ended in a Brownie Troop camping trip. My husband's sister went on the trip instead of me because she's a lot more outdoorsy and actually *likes* that stuff. For months, I had to listen to other mothers tell me how wonderful "Aunt Karen" was and how everyone loved that Jené brought her aunt on the camping trip. For some, that might have been bothersome, but I was just glad (and grateful) that we had an Aunt Karen so that I didn't have to be there.

One afternoon the following year, my daughter and I were in the car driving home from her dance studio. She asked me if she could sign up for Brownies again. I thought about it for a few minutes, considered the skills and traits that she would learn by being in the Brownies, and knew, of course, that I only wanted what was best for her. We were at a stop sign, and I looked at her and said, "Honey, of *course* you can be a Brownie again if that's what you want. But I tell you what—I'll give you $100 cash right now if you decide to say no." She thought about it for a few minutes, and she said, "I'll take the $100."

That's my girl.

Our last nanny stayed with us for seventeen years—for five of those years, the girls did not even live at home. They had gone to (and graduated from) college. The oldest one had moved to Los Angeles. It seemed a bit much to have a nanny when we did not have kids, so we promoted her to house manager, which was basically the same job without the kids and a better title. She helped with everything except the cooking. She knew my house better than I did, and with all my travel, I know she spent more time there than I did.

When I finally told my friends our house manager still came in five days a week, I got all kinds of grief, but you know what? I made my decision. I *owned* it. I made no apologies for it. Several months ago, when she resigned so that she and her husband could open a restaurant, I nearly had a panic attack. I was, and am, so happy for her, of course, and I miss her terribly, but my first thought when she told me she was resigning was, "Well, who the hell is going to do all that stuff *now?*" I quickly sprang into action: I ordered a robotic vacuum thingy to sweep the floors, and then I bought one that could mop the floors, too. (Neither of those gadgets get much use, but at least we have them!) We are figuring out the whole chore thing. My husband is like a military general; at least that is my perspective. He would probably describe himself as "just tidy," and he'd also say that I am not (and he'd be right), but somehow we're making it work. I guess that's another life lesson: *you do what you have to do to make it work.*

I have found that you have to make conscious decisions to *not* do something at work and deal with the consequences so that you could do something at home instead, and the other way around. It's more of a trade-off than a balance. It is hard being a working parent, and it is even harder if you constantly question your choices, so do not do that to yourself. Every working parent I know is doing the best they can and, really, that is all anyone can ask for.

I think it is getting easier as more companies are offering flex-time schedules and paid time off in many cases, which gives workers more options than just sick leave and vacation time. Women no longer feel like they have to make up an excuse for leaving the office early because they have to take their child to a medical appointment. It is easier now when your child is sick and you cannot get to that important meeting. With new technologies, men and women can work from home. And the unwelcome arrival of COVID-19 brought with it drastic changes in workplace and telecommuting patterns in a way that will forever redefine the notion of working from home. This is all to say: we are closer than ever to getting the best of both worlds—almost.

The key to all of this, as I said at the very beginning, is not to balance it but to *own it*.

CHAPTER TWELVE

STOP TELLING ME YOU DON'T SEE COLOR OR GENDER

" You cannot swim for new horizons until you have the courage to lose sight of the shore."

WILLIAM FAULKNER

I've learned a lot in the four years since I've had cancer. I have shared many of these lessons with you in various chapters of the book. I wish I could boil these nuggets of wisdom and experience down to one key message, but I can't. Not yet. In fact, now that I think about it, I realize that these lessons maybe aren't meant to be distilled down to one larger lesson at all. Maybe they are *meant* to be distinct; separate threads that you can hopefully weave throughout the fabric of your own life.

What I do know with certainty is this: I am both pleased and sad-dened that after the fifteen or so years I've been developing and refin-ing these lessons, they are just as true, just as raw, and just as relevant as they were when I first learned them. I guess that's what wisdom is: truth that endures. And because these lessons have stuck with me, I am equally hopeful that they will stick with you, too. I am fully and fiercely committed to continue spreading their wisdom and shining the light of knowledge on as many people as I possibly can. I will continue to give speeches and talks about these life lessons because they are important for women, for minorities, and especially for female minorities because we, more than most, are losing ground.

I think I'm getting grumpy in my old age. There was a time when people told me that they did not think of me (or even see me) as Black or as a woman, but simply as "Charlene." At the time, it *felt* like a compliment. I almost always said, "Thank you." But these days, such "color-blind" and "gender-blind" statements irritate me no end.

When a person says they don't see color or gender, you can bet that color and gender are *exactly* what they see and all the systemic biases that go with it. I mean, you don't comment about something you don't *see*, do you? Correct me if I'm wrong, but isn't it a little difficult to devote much attention to something that isn't supposed to even be registering? If anything, when people say they don't see color or gender, it tells me that they *do* see it; that it *is* on their radar, and that my gender and my Blackness have indeed played a role in how they perceive me. Why else would they have mentioned it?

I guess I can't call this grumpiness.

I can, and do, call it clear-sighted realism.

Further, when someone says (I assume innocently) that they don't see color or gender when they see me, my immediate thought is, "Then you don't see me." I always tell them that I *want* them to see my color and my gender because these are the characteristics that help make me who I am. I want them to understand that these characteristics are not a reason to discount me. I want to succeed, and I want you, dear reader, to succeed as whoever you are and at whatever you want to be. I believe that some of the issues surrounding the topic of women and minorities in the workplace can be tied back to not being seen, to this entire notion of corporate invisibility, which is the primary (if not sole) reason I gave my highly popular lecture series the moniker, "Lessons from Being Invisible."

There is a lot that can be said about women and minorities in the workplace, and I doubt that much of it is new. Although, over the last decade or so, it has certainly become more encouraging if you are a woman, but only slightly more encouraging if you are a woman of color. When Sheryl Sandberg, COO of Facebook and founder of LeanIn.Org, wrote *Lean In: Women, Work, and the Will to Lead*, she awakened a movement about women in the workplace of today. But even before Sandberg, the Catalyst organization, which began in 1962, put a stake in the ground with its mission to accelerate progress for women through workplace inclusion. That was more than fifty-five years ago. (Catalyst is a global nonprofit working with some of the world's most powerful CEOs and leading companies to build workplaces that work for women—see www.catalyst.org.)

I applaud Catalyst and other organizations like it for taking up the challenge for women around the world. Even so, we must ask ourselves how much progress has really been made since Catalyst began almost sixty years ago? Six decades certainly seems like more than enough time to reach equality, doesn't it? It turns out that that is not enough time for our nation or our world. Yes, progress has been made—but it has been slow. Hopefully, the days when we had to make a case for (and a fuss over) diversity are over. It has been proven again and again that companies that embrace diversity outpace the performance of those that don't. So, what's the problem?

When I started in the workforce in the late 1980s, it was the first time I'd heard about this thing called *diversity* and the lack of it being a problem in the workplace. At the ripe old age of twenty-two, I had a job—a good one, too—and that is pretty much all I cared about. In the beginning, I was not bothered because, as I mentioned earlier in this book, I really had no expectation of fairness or equality. And, my first boss was a Black woman. I had no idea what she faced as the only Black female executive in this massive business complex we worked within, but even then I knew it could not have been easy. As I grew older and bolder, I began to ask questions about why there weren't more people who looked like me. More often than not, I was told that it was a "pipeline" issue, meaning that there just weren't enough smart women and minorities seeking these white-collar executive jobs, so how could we expect to see women and minorities in leadership and executive positions?

> Let's stop trying to convince ourselves—and worse, stop deluding other people—into thinking that this is a pipeline issue. It's not. Let's just acknowledge that in many companies and in many industries, *systemic bias is the issue.*

I was willing to accept that explanation for a while; honestly, I didn't know any better. Is it possible that this is *still* a pipeline issue? Many companies will tell you yes. Well, I am just going to call bullshit on that. Are we really to believe that in more than thirty years the pipeline has not expanded? Haven't all those people who were in the pipeline thirty years ago grown up yet? Especially given the fact that the number of women earning college degrees outnumbers men. At a time when more people of color than ever are earning college degrees, we still have a pipeline issue? Let's stop trying to convince ourselves—and worse, stop deluding other people—into thinking that this is a pipeline issue. It's not. Let's just acknowledge that in many companies and in many industries, systemic bias is the issue.

In general, the system was built to favor White men—and it still does. I am fortunate to have worked at a few companies that have been considered diversity leaders and today would be lauded as being ahead of the game on diversity, equity, and inclusion. I applaud these companies because I believe they are operating from a considerably basic reality: that although talent and intelligence is equally distributed, opportunity is not. As a result, they are actively working to correct the shortfalls in their organizations. Although I celebrate these companies and their progress, my experiences, both personal and professional, remind me that the fatigue of exclusion is still a burden that is felt by many and leaving us weary.

We now have more women in senior executive positions at Fortune 500 companies than ever before in the United States. Still, according to *Fortune* magazine, in 2020, there are approximately three women of color who serve as CEOs today. As we know all too well, not every woman experiences the workplace in the same way. Catalyst also noted in their April 2020 report, *CEOs in Underrepresented Groups*, that women of color hold less than 13 percent of management jobs, and Black women hold fewer than 4 percent of management positions in the S&P 500.

The numbers are better when we consider that in 2019 there were thirty-three women CEOs in Fortune 500 companies, according to *Fortune* magazine. This is dismal, but promising. The first Black woman to ever serve as CEO of a Fortune 500 company was Ursula Burns, CEO of Xerox from 2009 to 2017. I have never met Ms. Burns, but it is impossible to not smile when I think of her accomplishment. Today, there are only four Black CEOs, and they are all men, according to *Business Insider* magazine. Clearly, White women are shattering the glass ceiling, but Black women are still running into the concrete wall.

Surely, we can do better.

It turns out that we may not. Since I started writing this book, several significant situations have unfolded ("exploded" might be the better descriptor) around the world that make me wonder about, well, almost *everything*. As of this writing, the United States is a hot spot for the global pandemic of the novel coronavirus, the virus that leads to COVID-19. Again, as of this writing, the nation has more than ten million cases across the country, and in more than 100,000 people have died. For the last three months of writing this book, citizens across the nation and the world have been told to stay off the streets and remain inside their homes. Businesses large and small—many of them considered iconic mainstays in American culture—are filing for bankruptcy protection, and some may never open again. Minorities and women are disproportionately affected by the health and economic fallout from COVID-19. Black people are dying at twice the rate as Whites. People wear face masks to protect themselves from the virus, and some states have even mandated that masks must always be worn in public spaces. With COVID-19, we have all learned new terminology and new ways to be together, including "social distancing," where no two people who are not living together should stand no closer than six feet apart. No hugging, handshaking, dapping, or anything else that would result in human contact. If I didn't know better, I would think I was living in a science-fiction movie. And as if that isn't enough, the United States is also in the midst of *another* kind of pandemic—perhaps even more powerful—the pandemic of blatant, undeniable, racial injustice.

Protests and riots are playing out with a frequency and a ferocity that we haven't seen since the 1960s. It is really sobering stuff, and this, too, has brought things to a screeching halt in our country. There are protests and riots in cities large and small, not just in the United States, but in other countries, as well. It's a very clear signal that enough is enough.

While history might say the original impetus was police brutality and a blatant disregard for Black life, the issue has become far more expansive and has shined a light on the overall state of race relations in America. Unfortunately, this brighter light reveals the dark, disturbing and, yes, devastating underbelly of racism and bigotry in America today. And one thing has become very clear: It is not now, nor has it ever been, a good time to be a Black person in America.

You might think that this makes me feel a complete loss of hope. But that's the thing about Black people: we're resilient, we understand struggle, and through all that happened to our race (the bondage, despicable brutality, outright disdain and disrespect, and our despair, unimaginable poverty, and lack of equality), we as a people remain hopeful and strong. Because we have hope. Not just hope for Black people, but hope for everyone, for our nation, and ultimately, for our world. Hope keeps us believing that a better time will come.

Race and gender are with me every day. And there are things I'd like the privilege of doing that I don't know that I'll ever achieve—either because things won't change, or that if they do, I'll be so mentally imprisoned by repeated biases that I can't see the difference.

I want to see women and especially minorities get their fair share of everything in the workplace. Perhaps the current state of our nation will accelerate change, but it could just as easily stall it. The "new normal" we all thought we'd be walking into once the coronavirus was under control has been completely upended. As this plays out, we once again have to wonder if this will help or hurt women and minorities in the workplace in the long run. What is it going to take for us to achieve equity? Not just inclusion, but *belonging* as well? White men created this problem, and I believe that ultimately, White men must have a major hand in fixing it.

But that does not mean we should give up. It is time for us to put on our Big Girl Pants and *lead* this fight. We are warriors. We can *do* this. And rather than only demanding equality for women, let's call out the laziness and sense of entitlement and privilege that so often comes from incompetent men. A recent *Harvard Business Review* article written by Tomas Chamorro-Premuzic and Cindy Gallop said it best: "The real problem is not a lack of competent females; it is too few obstacles for incompetent males, which explains the surplus of overconfident, narcissistic, and unethical people in charge."

Let us think on that one for a while.

Author's note: As I read through this manuscript before it is sent to the printer, news outlets have reported that Senator Joe Biden has become the forty-sixth president-elect of our nation, and standing at his side, Senator Kamala Harris has made history as the first female vice president-elect—and the first woman of color/Black woman—to ascend to this position. I never thought that in my lifetime this would be possible. In her first speech as vice president-elect, she confidently stated that while she is the first woman to hold this office, she won't be the last. Like I said earlier in the book, it starts with one.

Our nation has had a tough few years, and 2020 seemed the culmination of nearly everything that could go wrong. At times over the past few years, and especially the past few months, it seemed to me that hate and divisiveness reigned supreme in the United States. We still have a long way to go, but today, I am even more hopeful about women and minorities and our ability to achieve. Today, love won over hate. As I fully absorbed the enormity of the moment, I realized that I had been holding my breath for months wondering if Black lives really mattered. And today, I exhaled. For the first time in a long time, I could breathe. So, yes, while this author's note might be timely and topical, its timelessness is what makes it most significant.

SUPERSTITION

I'm superstitious. There is no Chapter Thirteen.

CHAPTER FOURTEEN

CANCER CHANGES YOU

" What makes you vulnerable
makes you beautiful."
BRENÉ BROWN

Cancer has had a lot to do with who I am today and with who I have become.

Through cancer, I have learned to be vulnerable, therefore, as Brené Brown says in the opening quote, I have learned a new way to be beautiful. I'm not talking about external beauty, but *internal* beauty; the kind that lives deep, deep down in my soul. People almost always say cancer is a journey. I have said it many times myself, but it isn't until now, nearly four years after my diagnosis, that I really and fully understand what that means. It is a journey to a place that is different, sometimes unpleasant, but almost always it leads to a more impactful way of life.

Cancer has changed me for the better. I am in a better place with my life. Going back and reading my blog posts, I see the growth process I was in that I just wasn't aware of at the time. Although my blog posts appear throughout this book and you can still access my blog online (www.justbetweenusgirrls.com), there are three blog posts I want to share with you here. To me, they show there is strength in weakness and a courage that comes from fear, whether that fear springs from life challenges, health crises, or career obstacles. I count these three blog posts among my favorites. These posts, along with the others, helped me find my way back to myself. And they helped me create the life I wanted.

The very life I'm living now.

This first blog entry was written after radiation ended, the beginning of my realization that I would never be the same again and that I needed to come to terms with what had happened to me.

Cancer has changed me for the better. I am in a better place with my life. Going back and reading my blog posts, I see the growth process I was in that I just wasn't aware of at the time.

◆ ◆ ◆

I Knew I Hit Rock Bottom When I Bought a Mink Coat

JULY 26, 2018

I'm depressed. I've been dealing with depression most of my life, so I know it when I see it. My mom had it, and so did her mother. I have some rather good coping mechanisms, but they aren't working this time.

If you watched my video "Why Not?" you might have noticed that my right false eyelash was starting to come off. The old me would have reshot that video as many times as necessary to get it perfect. But the new me doesn't really give a shit about a half-glued eyelash today. Because when you have cancer, shit happens; some of it you deal with, and some you just have to let go. That's how I know I'm depressed: that's just not me. My goal is always perfection when it comes to my appearance. Superficial, maybe, but I own it.

I really dislike fur clothing. Yes, it looks elegant. But is it worth some cute, little animals being clubbed to death so I can stay warm? Nope. Fur is not for me. I have been anti-fur for as long as I can remember. I have friends who have gorgeous mink coats. I don't judge my friends for wearing fur; I just ask them to make sure their fur doesn't touch me.

So, why is there a mink coat hanging in my closet?

When I'm depressed, I shop. It's what I do. Some people eat, some people retreat into themselves, I shop. I had finished cancer treatment almost two months earlier. I had a great Christmas holiday with my family, and we were all feeling so thankful that I made it through my treatment plan and a few unexpected complications. I still had reconstruction ahead of me, but, hey, a new set of breasts is like the pot of gold at the end of the rainbow. So, why was I down? Cancer started the battle, but I had finished it. *Hadn't I?*

Confident a quick trip to the mall would make it all okay, I bought a few things. As I headed out the door, the fur shop caught the corner of my eye. A store I would never be caught walking into before, but today I thought, "There's no harm in looking or even trying on a few." Other customers in the store were telling me that I looked great. So, this was it. A mink coat would brighten my spirits. I teared up when I bought the coat wondering, *What am I doing here?* The salesperson thought I was emotional about buying my first one. She said, "Your first mink is always special." She asked me if I wanted my initials stitched into the inside because that's what people do. I said no, it wasn't necessary. I wanted no proof that the coat belonged to me.

Even as I gently laid the bag in my trunk, I started to feel a knot in my stomach. By the time I got in the car, I started mentally reviewing the cost of "feel-good" purchases I had made that week. I had spent a little over $100,000. I don't have $100,000, and I especially don't have it to throw around. And to top it off, I was still depressed. I still cried. I still felt empty. I told myself to quit being a wimp and put on my Big Girl Pants and be an adult. No one has time for all this feeling sorry for yourself.

I went to see a psychiatrist. I expected him to tell me or give me the magic fix. I told him about my spending, that I don't have much energy or care about much, that the hot flashes are killing me, and that I am not happy. He asked me if spending $100,000 in a week was unusual for me. Isn't it unusual for everyone? I told him I had fantasies of killing myself. He asked me if I ever would, and I said no because my faith prevents me from committing such an act. By the end of the appointment, satisfied I wasn't going to harm myself, he prescribed an antidepressant (for the hot flashes) and told me not to worry, I would be just fine. After all, I had just kicked cancer. I'm a strong person. I should be thrilled, he said. I smiled and said, "Of course I am." It was a lie, but it was clearly what he needed to hear.

I returned what I could of the things I purchased, which was almost everything. I haven't returned the mink coat: it was a final sale.

I was speaking to a friend whom I met in treatment. She confided in me that she, too, was feeling off. She finished treatment months before me, so did that mean I had months of depression ahead of me? Months of pretending to be happy and telling people how lucky I am that they found the cancer early, only in one breast, and just Stage 2? For how much longer would I have to keep up the facade? It's exhausting! Were my friend and I unique in our feelings?

When people prepare you for your battle with cancer, they are helping you get the right attitude to fight for your life. But who is helping us afterward when we don't know what life we're fighting for anymore or maybe fighting for a life we don't want?

I still have that mink coat. I don't know why I haven't sold it or gotten rid of it. Every time I look at it hanging in the closet, I feel bad. Sometimes I try it on, and then I feel worse. When I told my twenty-four-year old daughter about the coat (she's also anti-fur), she looked at me and said, "Is it okay that I'm disappointed in you?" Those words cut like a knife. Maybe I will keep the coat to remind me that in disappointing my kid, I realized I was disappointed in myself for trying to cure something broken inside with something I could only wear on the outside—just another disguise while I hide from the truth—life after breast cancer sucks.

One area people are often afraid to talk about before, during, and especially after breast cancer is the insecurities that develop and the fear that sets in around your body, your body image, and whether or not your significant other sees you in the same way or even wants you in the same way. Trust me. Cancer changes everything.

◆ ◆ ◆

I Do, Take Two

My husband and I have had this "thing" for the past several years about renewing our vows. It started as we approached our twenty-year anniversary, and I suggested it. His response was swift and definitive: "No, I did it once, and I don't need to do it again. Besides, you only want to do it so you can have a big party and be the center of attention."

Well, truth be told, he wasn't wrong.

The next time it came up was when we were married for twenty-five years. Through a massive communications breakdown between Greg, one of my daughters, and me, I was under the impression that he wanted to renew our vows. I did what any woman would do if she could—I ordered a custom-made dress. Even though I had that beautiful dress, I just wasn't feeling it that year. When I told him I wasn't feeling a vow renewal, he just shrugged and asked where I had gotten the idea to begin with. My daughter, of course.

This year marks the twenty-seventh year we have been married. Now I'm feeling it—because it's AC (after cancer), and things that once didn't matter so much now seem to matter a lot. He was open to it but thought we should wait for a big anniversary, like our thirtieth. It makes sense, of course, but I couldn't get comfortable with it. How could I tell him that we had to do it this year because deep down I thought I might not be alive in three years? I didn't want to say that aloud, but I was definitely thinking it. Perhaps he picked up on it on his own, I don't know, but we agreed that we would have a vow renewal, just the two of us, on the beach.

Fast forward a few months, and I asked him something about the arrangements, and he responded quickly but nicely: "Do what you want, I'm only doing this to make you happy." Now, I know many women who would say, "Wow, he is doing this just so that I'm happy!" and be ecstatic about it. I'm not one of them. I don't exactly know how to describe my response, but let's just say I went bat-shit crazy and canceled the renewal. My rationale was that a vow renewal was like a wedding of sorts, and you don't get married just to make your partner happy. *Right?*

I took one more run at it a couple of weeks later when we were in a place where we could have a serious talk—the car. I told him I was going to ask him a serious question and he had to give me a truthful answer, no matter how uncomfortable it made him. I said that he could take his time, but he had to be honest. That this wasn't one of those questions like, "Do these jeans make my butt look big?" and he says no, but we both know they do. Anyway, the question. "After everything we've been through, and especially the last couple of years, would you marry me again?" I held my breath hoping for an answer sooner rather than later. Before I passed out, he said, "Yes, definitely." I said okay then, we'll renew our vows.

I decided to unpack why this vow renewal was so important to me, even putting aside the timing issue. I guess you don't have to be a renowned psychiatrist to figure this one out. But it took me some time. I'm not an insecure person, usually. Before cancer, I was very confident in myself—sometimes overly so. After cancer, sometimes I'm almost the exact opposite: shrouded in self-doubt.

When I met my husband, I was twenty-seven years old, an NFL cheerleader with a cute, size-two figure that I did absolutely nothing to maintain; it was just natural. I had tons of energy and never met a party I didn't like. Dammit, I was fun!

Over time, I changed, but not that much (at least, I don't think so, but Greg might think differently). Clearly, I'm not an NFL cheerleader anymore; we have children who are adults now; I'm still up for a party, but only if it ends by 9:00 pm; and that size-two figure? Well, two years ago, it was a size four to six, which wasn't so bad, but today it's a wreck. I have scars, lots of them. I have fat in strange places that I don't remember having a year ago. I didn't know then that the average breast cancer patient gains 15–20 pounds during treatment. That would have been nice to know. I would have eaten less ice cream. *Maybe.* I thought cancer patients were supposed to be skinny! Turns out, it depends on what kind of cancer you have.

My one-and-a-half boobs (remember, I'm still awaiting re-reconstruction, and I have a tissue expander on the left and an implant on the right) are really lopsided. I mean, *really.* One is a full inch higher than the other one. The half-boob points down and to the left, the whole one points up and to the right, and I think it's starting to sag. My doctor said something about needing a breast lift on that side. Really? From great boobs to no boob, to sagging boob, to breast lift? It's just ridiculous. And it's sad, too, at least to me. Needless to say, I have body-image issues.

Did you know that a married woman with a serious disease is six times more likely than a man to be divorced or separated before her treatment ends? The divorce rate increases by 50 percent when a woman gets a breast cancer diagnosis. It happens so often there's a term for it: partner abandonment.

After reading those stats and many more, I imagined myself in the midst of partner abandonment. I am a fifty-four-year-old woman with a body I barely want to show my doctor, let alone someone new. How do you tell someone new that you're not quite yourself physically? On a second date, over dessert? Nope, not me. Which meant only one thing: I was destined to grow old alone in a house full of dogs and useless things that I've hoarded over the years, and when I died, no one would know because the dogs would have eaten me because there was no dog food.

Okay, that is a bit dramatic, but I did start to worry about the rest of my life. Who would I date? Who would date me, assuming I would have the confidence to date? Men have more options as they get older. Women have fewer, and cancer patients even fewer still, maybe. Cancer leaves you feeling like damaged goods.

And that was the crux of the whole vow renewal thing. Fear. If my husband didn't want me, who would? If he didn't want to renew our vows, was it a signal of the beginning of the end? At times, I certainly thought so.

How in the hell did I become this person? If a friend gave me this sob story, I think I would slap her and say, "What the hell is wrong with you?"

What is wrong is that I had cancer. What is wrong is that cancer has taken more from me than it's given. What is wrong is that I wonder every day if one day I will be in the partner abandonment club. What is wrong is that I spend any time at all having these thoughts. It's not rational, but neither is this disease that you can never quite get away from.

Right about the time I started to circle the drain with these thoughts, my husband came upstairs and entered the room.

I looked up from my writing because I could feel him staring at me.

When I caught his eye, he looked at me and said ever-so kindly, "I choose you. Every day, I choose you."

P.S. We renewed our vows on September 10, 2018.

◆ ◆ ◆

This is the last post I wrote before writing this book. To me, it brings it all home.

◆ ◆ ◆

BLOG POST

Just One More Slice

FEBRUARY 8, 2020

I had another surgery in January; four weeks ago, in fact. I have now lost count of how many re-revisions of breast reconstruction I've had. I wonder how many surgeries you can have before the rest of your body breaks down; clearly, more than nine in three years. I read somewhere that every time someone goes under anesthesia, they lose a little bit of their memory. If it's true, that explains a lot (but not everything!).

In prepping for my surgery, the doctor informed me that he would have to do more fat grafting. A lot of people dislike fat grafting, but not me. Let's be real: if surgery is a must and the doctor is going to take fat from one place where I don't want it and put it in another place that needs it, that guy's a hero in my book. I mean, what is so bad about that? I will tell you. They never take it from where you want them to! My doctor and I have been through this dance before over the past two years. He says, "Where would you like me to take the fat from?" And I say, "Here, here, and here" pointing to various parts of my midsection and backside. Then he lets out a little sigh and says no, then reminds me that this is not cosmetic surgery; this is serious business. And he says it just like that, "This is not cosmetic surgery, Charlene." Pfft! I get it, but in this era where everything is negotiated, it didn't seem like too much to ask. Evidently, the fat in your midsection (which has a name, I just can't think of it right now) is there to protect your organs and keep them in place. Well, okay, since he put it like that. I gave in, fully realizing that I had no choice. But seriously, as long as he is in there.

So, on with the surgery, which was uneventful. Don't get me wrong, every time I am anesthetized and sliced into it gets a little more frightening. The last two times I had complications, which were not fun, so needless to say, I had a little trepidation. Mainly, for two reasons. 1. As always, I worry that I might not wake up, and 2. According to Greg, I say a lot of inappropriate things as I am coming out of anesthesia. Like, really inappropriate. Not "I've-had-too-much-to-drink-inappropriate"—worse. The kind of inappropriate that fully, people just stare at you when you wake up. I wonder if I curse like a sailor. I have always wanted to speak with lots of expletives just because I could. Greg stays mum about the whole thing, which means it must be bad. This time, though, I do recall him asking me who I loved more, him or the dogs. Duh, you can always find another husband. (Just kidding, honey).

I flew back to Houston this week for my post-op. One breast (the one that had cancer) is significantly larger than the other one (because of all the fat he put in there). He told me not to worry, though, because my body would absorb most of the fat, and if I'm lucky, it will shrink to match the other one. Wait. One. Minute. "Lucky?" WTF? At which point, he tells me that we will know in about three to four months if everything is fine and that he really doesn't want to cut into me again. I smile because I don't want him cutting into me again, either! Then he said, "You know, Charlene, you're a difficult case." (Like I have never heard THAT before; but wait—he was talking about my reconstruction). I nodded, and then he said something I will never forget. He said, "When you came in here the first time, after your breast exploded, you were one of the worst cases of reconstruction that I'd seen. Your situation was very, very, very, difficult."

Now, here is the deal. I know he is doing his best, and I am beyond thankful that my case landed in this particular doctor's caseload. But when a renowned reconstruction specialist says "very" not one, but three times, it means something. This surgeon is awesome and not one for hyperbole, so I realize then that in all this time that I've been agitating over these damn surgeries, he's been trying to solve a tough problem, working to make sure that his years of training and experience at MD Anderson and other places would come to bear to address "the worst case he's ever seen." Damn. I have always known that I'd make history one day, but this isn't how I thought it would happen—one slice at a time.

I am humbled. Still, the next slice I want to be a part of is one from a carrot cake on my birthday when I turn fifty-six in a few months. That should be right before I see him again for another post-op check in. Maybe I'll bring the cake, just to be sure.

Stay positive, friends.

P.S. That turned out to be my last surgery, and, yes, I had carrot cake on my birthday.

CHAPTER FIFTEEN

THIS WAS
MY STORY

" It took me quite a long time to develop a voice,
and now that I have it, I am not going to be
silent."

MADELEINE ALBRIGHT

By the time this book is published, I will be near the four-year mark of
my breast cancer diagnosis. What I remember most around that time was
my dual focus on not always asking God, "Why me?" but also wanting
desperately to know what God was trying to teach me. Through a thirty-
plus-year career, I have learned plenty of important life lessons. You've
read them! But also, as a lifelong Christian, I believe that when something
bad happens to you, it happens for a reason, and you have a responsibility
(in this case, I had a responsibility) to turn a negative into a positive, not
just for me, but for the people around me. I know that doesn't explain

everything that happens in life—so many things seem inexplicable—but, nonetheless, this is how I make sense of my life. I've worked hard to keep an open mind over these past four years, waiting for the purpose, the reason, the rationale behind this cancer, to be revealed to me. I didn't expect the booming Voice of God to wake me up one day and say, "Charlene, *this* is why you have cancer." Rather, I knew deep down inside that the reason would slowly unfold, and it did. I have my answer.

The answer is this book. The answer is my new attitude. The answer is my new sense of peace and purpose. I now have a new voice—a voice that I didn't know I had (maybe because I didn't have it then, but I do have it now!), and it is a voice that I treasure. It's a willingness, a calling, to step up and step out with courage and conviction to tell my real story so that it might help others. To bring light to what it's like to walk in the shoes of someone who has been diminished, ignored, discounted, honored, celebrated, awarded, and admired.

This was not always an easy book to write. I'm sure that many readers will wonder why I shared some details of my life that may or may not be pertinent to the story, such as the abuse my mother suffered at the hands of my father, the sexual abuse I experienced as a little girl, and the depression I felt so strongly and desperately when the invasive aspects of my cancer treatment were completed. I chose to speak about those things to help bring them out of the darkness and into the light. It's only when things are brought to light that they can be addressed.

Throughout my journey, many people have referred to me as being strong, inspirational, admirable (their words, not mine). I think it's important for people to know that strong, inspirational, and admirable people suffer, too. We hurt. We question our value. We sometimes feel lost. We are not immune. Sharing these stories, reliving these experiences, recounting some of the raw elements of my journey, are not to gain sympathy from you, my readers. It's about helping people who don't feel strong see that even the strongest are weak; it's important to remember that even those who are inspirational sometimes need to be inspired. And, it's all okay.

A few months after I started my blog documenting my feelings during my relationship with cancer, someone I hold near and dear to my heart (who was going through her own challenges at the time) told me that she cried when she read a particular post I had written. It touched her. She empathized with me and what I was going through. By the time she finished reading it, she wasn't thinking about me anymore. Her focus was, properly, on her. She told me that if someone like me—who she considered a pillar of strength—could feel the way I did, then she needed to stop being so hard on herself; maybe, just maybe, she was okay, and her feelings of inadequacy were not warranted. *It's okay to not always be okay.* This is one of the most powerful things anyone has ever said to me.

So, my friend gained strength through my weakness. Through my vulnerability. And if I can do that for one person, then my prayer is that I can do that for you, my readers, as well. But, even more importantly, what I really hope is that I have encouraged you to speak your truth because by expressing (and living) your own truth, someone else may find theirs, and the ripple in the pond continues to emanate outward from there. Writing this book has allowed me to become the pebble in the pond. I feel tremendously blessed, honored, and proud to send the power of my waves and the wisdom of my lessons straight to you.

Through my "Lessons from Being Invisible" lecture series, I've tried to share the challenges that many of us face and will continue to face throughout our careers, and I've sought to share useful solutions that have helped me. And by understanding and unpacking some of these lessons yourself, and weaving the threads of their wisdom into the fabric of our own daily life, I hope that you will gain a newfound strength that you never knew you even had. I hope that you will carve out a career and life for yourself that may not always be easy but, more often than not, will *rest within your own control*. Now, you must take these lessons and make them your own. I am offering them to you as a gift.

These lessons belong to you now. They belong to all of us. Now *you* must be that pebble in the pond. Now you must create small waves of wisdom so that they emanate outward and eventually reach those on distant shores, especially those who feel marginalized, excluded, and invisible. Especially those who have hit a brick wall or haven't yet shattered (or even touched) that glass ceiling. And someday soon, you will encounter—just like I did—more than one person who will tell you that they've gained strength from your vulnerability.

If someone told me a year ago that I would be out of the corporate world, which is the only work world I know, that I would write a book, start my own business, and proudly (and sometimes loudly) share my story, I would not have believed them.

But here I am, standing strong. Here I am, more concerned about unapologetic authenticity than accomplishment. Here I am, no longer concerned about winning (or even playing!) the game of corporate politics but newly energized by finding my firm place in the world and invigorated by succeeding at what really matters: living my life with my purpose.

When I started my career in 1987, I gladly woke up every morning, got ready for work, and just before leaving my apartment, I would put on my invisible suit of armor. This was the special shield that would help me deal with the myriad micro- and macroaggressions that I would face, day in and day out. Figuratively, that suit of armor was heavy, as most suits of armor are, but it provided the protection I needed at the time. Fast forward several years, and I saw myself trading in that suit of armor for a superhero cape. By then, I was a working mother, and as most women know, when you're a working mother, you *have* to be a superhero to get things done, at work, at home—everywhere. Sure, I still needed my suit of armor—but I needed my cape more. I had worked with enough working mothers to know about the delicate balance I needed to try to achieve and maintain. To the highest degree possible, I was prepared.

However, I was not prepared for returning to my post-cancer life. When that time came, I found that I needed that old suit of armor again. I had to take it out of the closet and dust it off. It was heavier than I remembered, but no less necessary. What really bothered me, though, was that I needed the suit of armor *and* I needed my cape. My children were young adults by then, so I didn't need my cape as a working mother, but I still needed to be a superhero in other parts of my life—a life I no longer recognized and one that I wasn't sure I fit into anymore. I found, however, that the law of physics was not on my side. It's awfully hard to soar when you're weighed down. It's another no-win situation. Many, many women are treated for cancer and have little-to-no problem returning to work or returning to themselves. Not so for me.

> Within weeks, if not days, it was very clear to me that I was not up to the life I had spent so long building. It was time to pivot. I learned that I could put away the cape, and I could recycle the suit of armor. After all of my life, career, and cancer challenges, I'd learned the best lesson of all: I don't need a cape.

Within weeks, if not days, it was very clear to me that I was not up to the life I had spent so long building. It was time to pivot. I learned that I could put away the cape, and I could recycle the suit of armor. After all of my life, career, and cancer challenges, I'd learned the best lesson of all: I don't need a cape.

I don't need a shield, either, because through the weakness of cancer, I gained the strength to become the director of my life, instead of twisting myself into so many versions of myself that at times I became unrecognizable, even to myself.

Today, I lean on two undisputable truths:

1. I am a child of the most-high God, and,

2. I am enough!

I. Am. Enough.

WWW.CHARLENEWHEELESS.BIZ

 @CHARWHEELESS

 @CHARWHEELESS

 CHARLENE WHEELESS

 CHARLENE WHEELESS

NOTES

NOTES

NOTES

NOTES

NOTES